GLEN ALEX

Living Boundaries

Affirming Your Line in the Sand to
Preserve Your Health and Well-being

ISBN: 978-1-969463-61-7

WHAT OTHERS ARE SAYING ABOUT
GLEN ALEX AND THIS BOOK

"*Living Boundaries* is a masterpiece you will treasure. Glen Alex's deep dive into boundaries is both illuminating and inspiring. Readers are empowered to protect and nurture themselves on all levels, far beyond just saying 'No.' As a result, they will not only experience more peace in their lives but take control of creating their destinies on their own terms."

—Patrick Snow, Publishing Coach and International Best-Selling Author of *Creating Your Own Destiny* and *The Affluent Entrepreneur*

"As a recovering codependent, setting boundaries was one of the hardest, most mysterious, and absolutely important lessons I ever had to learn. Therefore, I welcome Glen Alex's new book *Living Boundaries* with open arms. This revolutionary approach to understanding boundaries will enlighten you on the role your intuition plays in what and who you can allow into your life and where you need to draw a line you will not cross. Beyond setting boundaries with others, Alex explores the importance of setting boundaries with ourselves by getting to know ourselves better and in deeper ways. As Alex clarifies, once we know our boundaries, we can live Shakespeare's advice 'To thine own self be true,' and in the process, experience the joy and fulfillment we were born to enjoy."

—Tyler R. Tichelaar, PhD and Award-Winning Author of *The Mysteries of Marquette*

"I find this wonderful book, *Living Boundaries,* a stroke of genius. Glen truly is an excellent, gifted writer not only for her words but for her ideas."

—Alice Rogers, Retired Entrepreneur

" 'Have you ever asked yourself 'Why does he keep doing that to me?' The answer is because they can.' Living Boundaries* guides* readers through some complex psychological concepts, relationship dynamics, and internal processes in a succinct, accessible, and no-nonsense way. Glen not only defines concepts, but expounds on them with relatable examples throughout. The quizzes and reflection questions allow readers to internalize the lessons in the book so they can walk away with a better understanding of themselves and their boundary journey ahead immediately."

— Mynesha Whyte, MA, LPC - DEI practitioner,
dance/movement psychotherapist, co-Founder and President of
Black Magic Association, Oakland, CA

"'As an educator for twenty-five plus years, I am pleased to recommend Glen Alex's book, *Living Boundaries*.' She has provided clear and concise strategies to understand how to set different kinds of boundaries in order to live contently. Alex's writing style is approachable in terms of vocabulary and length which make it a very reader friendly resource. This book allows each person to create their own set of boundaries that will work for their unique needs. I found it to be a helpful resource that reinforces my boundary choices as well as improving some of those that could use some maintenance."

— Alice Weiner, MS EDUC, Ventura, California,
Retired Educator

"The more I read *Living Boundaries*, the more I thought 'how great would it be to have *Living Boundaries* taught to students throughout their K through 12th curriculum'. The tools set forth in Glen's discussion such as, who, what, when, where and how long, ICAN, and the legitimacy and purpose of anger, fear, sadness, love, and joy, capsulized a lifetime of hard knock lessons into a few pages of wisdom! Think about it!!!

Check this out…a real time result of reading *Living Boundaries*…today on a call from someone who I would normally recoil in response to her yelling to get me to give in to her irrational demands, I said, *'If you can't speak to me in a calmer voice, then I can't hear a word you're saying'*. She hung up – I thought Great! Thank you, Glen!! I felt empowered enough to set boundaries on the basis in which she may engage in discussion with me.

Glen, thank you for the opportunity to read *Living Boundaries*. How cool is that to embrace and act on your spirit's calling!"

—Karen Heads, Certified Public Accountant

"The book *Living Boundaries* by Glen Alex is so insightful and inspiring personal boundaries with an impactful focus on nurturing oneself. The chapters are organized on defining boundaries, but recognizing healthy and unhealthy types of boundaries. She uses real life scenarios to show the reader boundary concepts and the importance of understanding, identifying, and affirming one's boundaries. Glen aimed to empower individuals to protect themselves, guide relationships, and showed how to set healthy boundaries in their life. As a licensed school counselor, this book is a great tool in the mental health industry."

—Casper Sesto, PhD, Author, School Counselor

"Few genres of literature so clearly communicate the personal epoch like self-help books, a form that combines personal cognition with instructions on how to become a renewed embodiment of an elevation of values and paradigms. In her second book, Glen Alex is revisiting a chapter from her first book (*Living in Total Health*) and unpacking what is necessary to create solid and fortified living boundaries. For this book, she emphasizes that 'the path to total health' is for everyone. This book is an everyday assessment tool using 'I CAN' concepts that can be revisited at every step of the need to enrich your health and happiness."

—Jeanne deMontagnac-Hall, LMT, BSMT, MDT

"Glen Alex is a true professional. From writing books to hosting a podcast to pursuing education to avid tennis player and to charity, she consistently shows care for everyone's mental and physical well-being through her various selfless acts. As a man, a father, and a human being, Glen Alex has inspired me in numerous ways. She's truly my role model in more ways than one!"

—Larry Duncan, Entrepreneur

"Boundaries, you've heard about boundaries. Perhaps you haven't taken time to learn how important boundaries are in your everyday life. Boundaries affect your mental, emotional, and relational well-being. Glen has provided pertinent information pertaining to boundaries that must be established in order to maintain meaningful relationships. She provides relatable scenarios that are extremely helpful. We sometimes have expectations of others but don't express it to them.

As a result we are unhappy with them because they crossed a boundary that they didn't know anything about. Glen has included much thought-provoking information for readers to take a look at the boundaries they have established. Are they clear and known to others? I recommend *Living Boundaries*, as it truly is a must to add to your knowledge and literary collection.

Glen has created *Living Boundaries*, a very informative book that after reading you will truly understand boundaries. You will be able to make informed decisions regarding changes to what you have already established. The ultimate result is a happier you!"

—Cynthia Rapazzini, Ph.D., Author, School Counselor

"Glen Alex has accomplished a work of genius in her book *Living Boundaries*. The genius aspect is to make 'objective' this commonly subjective aspect of our lives. With vivid stories and illustrations from her own experience, Glen demonstrates that until we can objectify the 'what, why and how' of our personal boundaries, our ability to create healthy boundaries for ourselves is limited. Valuable information.

But Glen goes beyond giving us just another informational book. *Living Boundaries* is a workbook designed to guide the reader to understand the status of their own personal boundaries and then move beyond understanding to identify, strengthen and activate their boundaries in every relationship. Glen's book has been transformational in my own life.

Finally, *Living Boundaries* promises to have a more profound and wider effect than guiding the transformation of individual lives. Clarifying and maintaining one's personal boundaries is an action that has a positive, healthy influence on all relationships and society as a whole. Thus individual transformation, one person at a time, can be a key to activating a powerful transformation of society and of our world."

—David Smith, M-Div | Las Vegas, Nevada | Writer, Speaker,
Author, Digital Marketer and Creator of
https://LasVegasAreaTrails.com

"Healthy boundaries are not walls. They are gates and fences that allow you to enjoy the beauty of your own garden."

—Lydia Hall

DEDICATION

To my late father,
John Paul Whyte,

for his resolve to do the right thing, accept diverse individuals, treat himself and others with respect, and require others to treat him respectfully.

I recall his life lessons with great clarity. My father's loving influence has and continues to have a strong influence in my life and my work.

ACKNOWLEDGMENTS

It is with my deepest sincerity that I extend gratitude and appreciation to those individuals who have been and still are instrumental in my journey to wealth. While I've known some of them my entire life, others for much of my life, and others for shorter periods of time, their impact on my path is timeless and profound. I am so blessed with their authentic nurturing and support.

The list of those loving human beings is long and could be a book itself. I do thank each and every one of them from my heart. And I give special thanks to those whose encouragement and guidance had the most impact on my writing this book:

Ethel Mays
Benjamin Schiessl
Gwendolyn West
Alice Rogers
Joy Landers
Miss O'Malley
My Siblings
Young Glen Alex

Thank you.

Table of Contents

INTRODUCTION

Setting Healthy Boundaries Is a Human Issue

"Ultimately, boundaries are incredible gifts that we can offer to ourselves and the people in our lives. Boundaries empower us to choose how we want to relate and respond. When we are honest with ourselves and others, we create greater depth, meaning, and reciprocity in our relationships."
—Amy Vigliotti, Ph.D.

Living Boundaries…what on earth is that about? You may be asking yourself this question. The answer is that I believe interpersonal boundaries are alive, like living plants are. Boundaries live within you and are not separate from your person as pop culture suggests. This is a new way of understanding boundaries and living through them. My goal in writing this book is for you to connect with your *Living Boundaries* to have your most authentic loving and joyful life experience, so please read on.

Where did this come from? Another question to be answered. Well, my life's work is about total health and my journey in the health space began with boundaries. Growing up, our home was a social focal point. We often had parties and gatherings with family, neighbors, and friends. As a child, I was so captivated by the nuance of interaction—the tone of voice, when a person smiled or cringed, when pain crossed someone's face, and when their eyes lit up. I saw boundaries respected and boundaries violated in real time, and it stuck with me. I clearly remember vowing to never be the one to cause another person pain by being the aggressor, while understanding that self-defense would be appropriate at times. And so I went from witnessing boundaries, to learning boundaries, to living boundaries, and now to teaching boundaries. From there, my work expanded to other areas of health and I developed a unique and no-nonsense perspective to help others lead their healthiest and most joyful life. Thus, boundaries for me are the path to health and happiness.

And here we are with *Living Boundaries.* So at this point, allow me to be clear. One problem I see with boundaries is not with boundaries themselves. This problem with boundaries is with the *perception* of boundaries. The too common view of boundaries is that they exist outside of us, as if they are accessories that we don ourselves with or that which we grab hold of for a false sense of security. Not only are boundaries perceived as something we reach for with one word--too many people falsely believe that boundaries are only about saying *"no"*, or are something that you use pro re nata (PRN), as needed, like a pill for a headache. I present to you, however, that boundaries are so much more than a cloak or pill or simple utterance of the word *"no"*. Setting and maintaining healthy boundaries is how assertively and confidently you carry yourself in life, and they require a process of mindful self-awareness long before *"no"* becomes necessary.

Healthy boundaries are not idle tools waiting for you to pick up and use. There is no wrench to tighten up your physical well-being. There is no hammer to pound in your emotional or mental health. And there is no snake to twist reality to fit your comfort zone. Your boundaries are not an ace-in-the-hole. Another way to think of it is you wear your boundaries, like you carry your facial expressions, your gestures, your posture.

Another problem I see with boundaries is that women are held solely responsible for having them. However, the Women's Suffrage Movement, the National Organization for Women, and more recently the MeToo movement highlighted how unhealthy interpersonal boundaries are a human problem. This means that men, abusers, politicians, law enforcement, oppressors, the rich, and anyone who has power and authority over the lives and wellbeing of other human beings are equally, if not more responsible for developing, setting, and maintaining healthy boundaries. Just imagine *how wonderful this world would be* if all leaders, policy makers, enforcers, and business owners individually and collectively had healthy boundaries and did the right things? I submit to you that *Living Boundaries* are the path to total health for individuals, for society, and for humanity.

To sum up, *Living Boundaries* is about how your boundaries exist with your every breath, your every *no*, and with your every *yes*. Your boundaries are akin to your skin, your heart, your aura, your essence, and every other part of your being. You cannot detach from your boundaries. And so, healthy boundaries are your built-in, undeniable, personal alarm system which is monitored by your intuition and is available to you 24 hours per day, 7 days a week. Interpersonal boundaries are alive. Boundaries live and breathe with and within you as such. Thus, boundaries are an integral part of who you are and cannot be separated from your living being.

Your boundaries are alive. *Living Boundaries* expands upon the information presented in my first published book, the 5-time award winning *Living In Total Health*, particularly the Boundaries chapter. *Living In Total Health* covered the definition, purpose, types, and signs of unhealthy boundaries. *Living In Total Health* also introduced Wellth, which is health plus other riches and presents as being joyful, connected, confident, and complete. In *Living Boundaries,* your boundaries become more personally applicable to empower you to nurture and to protect yourself, setting the foundation for you to be wellthy. This incarnation of boundaries also includes assessments, exercises, activities, and real life examples of healthy and unhealthy boundaries to help you better understand how critical boundaries are to health and happiness so you can protect and nurture the integrity of who you are.

Please be aware that references to and examples of abuse and domestic violence are mentioned throughout this book, so proceed with caution.

Wearing your boundaries as a second skin provides you with an extra layer of protection and strengthens you to act in your own, most healthy interest.

FOREWORD
BY CYNTHIA RAPAZZINI, PH.D.

LIVING BOUNDARIES EMPOWER YOU

"Boundaries are the path to self-empowerment."
—themindresearchfoundation.org

Glen has written an interesting and informative book about boundaries. When I agreed to read and review *Living Boundaries*, I had no expectations. When reading this book what I discovered is that it resonated with me. Glen shared life experiences from her heart to give readers insight so they could feel what she was conveying.

As I read *Living Boundaries*, I became more interested because I was learning. In this powerful book, I didn't expect that the information would apply to me. Establishing boundaries is important in all relationships. You will find the information very helpful in establishing boundaries that are necessary. It's never too late if both parties in the relationship are willing.

Living Boundaries is a thought-provoking book. Glen has provided examples and experiences for readers to really consider. Think about what you're experiencing in your relationship. What is working? What is not working? What are you willing to change? Are you committed to the relationship? This is where you have to be honest.

When you read this *Living Boundaries* book you will realize that the examples Glen shared are real life experiences and strategies that you can use to establish new boundaries. Are you the go to person at work because you always help out and get the job done? Are you the one at work late regularly without monetary consideration? Do you take work home? Perhaps that needs to change? You do it now because it's the norm for you but it shouldn't be.

It requires you to just say NO, or I can't today, I have other obligations etc. It is difficult for many to say no but, that is what boundaries are for! Remember, it's not what you say, it's how you say it.

After reading *Living Boundaries* you will find a change in your mindset. You will be empowered to establish your New Boundaries Amazing Journey!

SECTION I:

DEFINING BOUNDARIES

CHAPTER 1

ASSESSING YOUR BOUNDARIES

"When you say 'yes' to others, make sure you're not saying 'no' to yourself."
—Paul Coelho

Let's assess your boundaries right off the bat. You see, a successful growth process always starts where you are. Not where you "should" be. Not even where you *want to be*. While your goals for your life are critical in directing your journey, they require you to get started. And that's where you are.

Use this Boundaries Assessment to assist you in better understanding the current status of your boundaries in the different areas of your life. Simply respond to the statements and questions below as honestly as you can. This is your starting point so the more genuine you are, the smoother your learning experience can be. Feel free to share your self-assessment with your therapist, counselor, or life coach to aid you in your process of setting and maintaining appropriate boundaries for your mental health and overall health.

Please keep in mind that this assessment is in no way about what's wrong with you. It is a learning opportunity to start your journey toward health and happiness.

1. Saying *no* makes you strong?
   □ Yes   □ No   □ It should

2. Boundaries only apply to sexual situations?
   □ Yes   □ No

3. Setting boundaries is the "in thing"?
   □ Yes   □ No

4. Having healthy boundaries help with stress?
   □ Yes   □ No   □ Makes stress worse

5. People will accept when you say *no?*
   □ Yes   □ No   □ They should

6. Do you overcommit to what family and friends want?
   □ All the time   □ A lot   □ Sometimes   □ No

7. Do you have trouble separating your thoughts and emotions from someone else?
   □ All the time   □ Sometimes   □ Never

8. Do you allow people to stand closer than you're comfortable with?
   □ Yes   □ No   □ Sometimes

9. Do you provide more information than the conversation requires?
   □ All the time   □ Sometimes   □ Never

10. How often do you apologize for being late or not following through on something?
    □ All the time   □ A lot   □ Sometimes   □ Rarely

11. Are you an open book?
    □ Yes   □ No

12. How often do you give in and do something you don't want to do?

□ All the time □ Sometimes □ Never

13. Does how people treat you align with your beliefs and values?

□ Yes □ No

14. How comfortable are you saying "no"?

□ Very □ Somewhat □ Not at all

15. How do you handle unwanted touching?

□ Back away □ Speak up □ Wait for it to end

16. Do you follow someone else's lead when you don't want to?

□ All the time □ Sometimes □ Never

17. People who care about you should know what you want and need?

□ Yes □ I think so □ No □ I'm not sure

18. Do you agree just to get along?

□ All the time □ A lot □ Sometimes □ Rarely

19. Do you sacrifice your self-care to do what others want you to do?

□ All the time □ A lot □ Sometimes □ No

20. Do you have trouble making time for self-care?

□ Yes □ No □ Sometimes

In reviewing your responses, answer the following questions:

What did you learn about yourself?

_____

What surprised you?

_____

What confirmed what you already knew or were told about yourself?

_____

What are your strengths?

_____

Which boundaries need improvement?

_____

This assessment will serve you further later on.

CHAPTER 2

DEFINING YOUR BOUNDARIES

*"Guard your heart, mind and time. Those three
things will determine the health of everything else in
your life."*
—Andrena Sawyer

YOUR INNATE ALARM SYSTEM

What are boundaries? Collectively, boundaries comprise your innate alarm system which is monitored by your intuition—your inner wisdom. Please focus on the words *innate* and *intuition* because you are born with boundaries and intuition; thus, both are ingrained in who you are and are available to you 24 hours per day, 7 days a week (24/7). I expand on intuition in Chapter 8, Intuiting Your Boundaries and Relationships. No one can separate you from your boundaries, from your inherited armor. As such, your boundaries alert you when you are in danger from another person and when you're in a perilous situation.

Even though your boundaries are innate and ever-present, you can, however, disconnect from or ignore them. Disconnection is often triggered by issues such as fearfulness, mental and emotional restriction, and abusive or unfulfilling relationships. Ignoring or dismissing your boundaries is giving your personal power away, allowing someone else to define your reality and to dictate your narrative. One goal of *Living Boundaries* is to help you reconnect with and respect your innate armor so you can live fully. Another goal is for you to experience authentic love and joy. In short, *Living Boundaries* lead to wellth.

WHY YOUR BOUNDARIES EXIST

Whether aware of your boundaries or not, your innate alarm system has very specific purposes—to protect and to nurture you.

1. Protection

Quite simply, the number one purpose of your boundaries is to protect you. Your boundaries alert you when any aspect of your wholeness is in danger. You see, you are a physical, mental, emotional, and spiritual being. And every aspect of who you are matters. Ignoring or emphasizing any one of these aspects leaves you vulnerable to manipulation, abuse, and harm by self and others. The alarm bells triggered by your boundaries are designed to draw your attention to the situation that poses danger to you on any or all levels. Your intuition sets off those alarm bells whenever your boundaries are crossed or are in jeopardy. And when alerted, you then have the opportunity to assess the situation and choose the most appropriate action to take to be safe.

> *"...the root of the word 'intuition', tuere, means "to guard, to protect."*
> —Gavin De Becker

Your innate alarm system alerts you by generating strong physical sensations, a powerful knowing, and other signals to heighten your awareness about what is happening to, within, and around you. More details about the alarm bells and examples of them are provided in Chapter 6--Revealing Emotional Boundary Red Flags, Chapter 7--Seeing Physical, Mental, and Spiritual Boundary Red Flags, and Chapter 8-- Intuiting Your Boundaries and Relationships.

2. Nurturing

Boundaries are also crucial in individuation, which is necessary to nurture your uniqueness. Individuation is the process by which human beings learn to understand themselves and gain a more clear sense of self that is separate from parents, siblings, peers, and others around them. Individuation is necessary for each of us to become our own unique selves and to develop our inherent talents and gifts to share with the world. Think of individuation as the phase teenagers go through. They typically rebel against or pull away from the norms of their family, culture, etc., as they sort out who they are. This process may also involve the teen being more private, changing their appearance, and seeming to be self-absorbed.

Individuation clarifies where you begin and end and where another person begins and ends. Thus, appropriate individuation gives rise to a healthy adult who is mentally and emotionally balanced, who understands who they are, who is self-confident, who is self-reliant, who is resilient, and who is capable of good self-care. Poor individuation leads to many negatives that cause mental and emotional problems, including but not limited to anxiety, depression, enmeshment, self-harm, and insecurity. Those who don't individuate appropriately also experience a diminished quality of life due to needing to get approval and self-worth externally, from others. As such, individuation is intimately *involved* with emotional boundaries, which will be discussed further in Chapter 3-- Categorizing Your Boundaries and Chapter 6—Revealing Emotional Boundary Red Flags. Thus, self-care is a crucial element in the nurturing function of boundaries.

SUMMARY

If you have an alarm system in your home, your car, your office, or some other place or location you value, then you know the importance of protection. And if you support the best in other people, then you are aware of the significant impact of nurturing. So then please share with me what stops you from protecting and nurturing yourself?

Another example of the importance of healthy boundaries is driving. Do you check the rearview and side mirrors while driving? If yes, then why? Do you look ahead, to your right, and to your left while on the road? If yes, then why? At the risk of being audacious, I bet you engage in those actions to become aware of what is going on around you so you can act to protect yourself if necessary. You can turn or change lanes to avoid an oncoming car. You can slow down to avoid a pedestrian or animal that suddenly appears. You can change lanes if a car comes up too fast behind you. All of these actions serve to keep danger at bay.

Allow me to be clear…without healthy boundaries, i.e., activation of your innate alarm system, you will not know when you need to protect yourself from harmful forces and you will be unable to develop into your uniqueness and share your innate gifts and talents with humanity. Healthy boundaries protect the integrity of your person and nurture your uniqueness so that you can navigate through life to experience authentic love and joy as safely as possible. The place to start is understanding what boundaries are and assessing the current status of your boundaries.

"Boundaries are to protect life,
not to limit pleasures."
—Edwin Louis Cole

CHAPTER 3

CATEGORIZING YOUR BOUNDARIES

"Setting different types of personal boundaries helps you prioritize your physical and mental wellness and establish the foundation for various kinds of relationships."
—Masterclass

TYPES OF BOUNDARIES

For this work, I distinguish four types of boundaries that collectively represent your wholeness—physical, mental, emotional, and spiritual. Here is an overview of these types of boundaries.

1. Physical Boundary

The physical boundary is the easiest to grasp because it's about your body and what happens to it. This boundary involves touching, feeling, and sexuality. Your physical boundary is delineated by the frame of your body and your personal space, which is the amount of space surrounding your body that you need to feel safe. That safe space varies according to the person, to the context, and to cultural norms.

For example, personal space pre-pandemic was 3-6 feet among Americans. In densely populated countries like India, personal space is shorter. According to https://www.studysmarter.us/ and Wikipedia, intimate/personal, social, and public spaces have their own comfort zone that is identified below:

- Intimate/personal space is touching to 4 feet.

- Social space is 4 – 12 feet.
- Public space is 12 – 25 feet.

Keep in mind that the above general spacing will shift according to each person's comfort level, the situation they are in, and the culture they are from. One example is best friends may stand further than 4 feet apart when arguing, which is more like social spacing. In another example, the same friends may sit only a few inches apart when talking about personal problems.

Thus, your physical boundary involves your body and what happens to it, and your physical comfort zone in relation to other people, which is your personal space.

> For example, Edith and Josh work for the same company in different departments. They interact briefly and casually during breaks in the lunch room. When Edith learned that Josh's wife gave birth to their first child, she congratulated him with a familial hug. Josh was uncomfortable because they are not that close. Edith's hug, though celebratory, violated Josh's intimate/personal space and triggered his shoulders to hunch.

Please note that the hunching of Josh's shoulder is a physical indicator of his discomfort, alerting him that his physical boundary was crossed.

3.1 Physical Boundary Activity

What is your comfort zone? Identify how physically close you are comfortable with these individuals. Use the "Depends" option to note contextual variances if needed.

Spouse / Partner:
□ 0-4 feet
□ 4-12 feet
□ 12-25 feet
□ Depends on_____

Family Member:
□ 0-4 feet
□ 4-12 feet
□ 12-25 feet
□ Depends on_____

Friend:
□ 0-4 feet
□ 4-12 feet
□ 12-25 feet
□ Depends on_____

Coworker:
□ 0-4 feet
□ 4-12 feet
□ 12-25 feet
□ Depends on_____

Acquaintance:
□ 0-4 feet
□ 4-12 feet
□ 12-25 feet
□ Depends on_____

Stranger:
□ 0-4 feet
□ 4-12 feet
□ 12-25 feet
□ Depends on_____

* * *

2. Mental Boundary

The mental boundary may not be what you think. It is not about thoughts that run through your mind, specifically. Rather, the mental boundary is about agreements and expectations.

<u>Agreements</u>

When 2 or more people agree to pursue a common goal, an agreement is formed with each person committing to their role in that process. Realistic expectations that each person will do their part naturally follow. Keep in mind that agreements are contracts—verbal, written, legal, etc. and can involve seemingly innocuous situations such as dinner time, appointments with professionals, and just keeping your word.

Agreements are broken when one person unilaterally changes the terms of the contract without communicating their desire to change the terms or communicating when they have difficulty keeping it with whom they made the agreement. Thus, you have a betrayal. Any broken agreement can be experienced as a betrayal, which involves much more than sexual infidelity.

> For example, I scheduled a 20-minute consultation with a marketer to promote my business for 1:00-1:20pm. My expectation was that she would be on time because she set the schedule. However, she didn't call until 1:17. So, we rushed through the call because I had another appointment

right after. At the end of the call, this marketer said she would email a proposal within 2 days. It was 2 weeks later when I received her proposal. I chose to work with someone else because of her betrayal in keeping her word--being on time and sending her proposal when she said she would. I did not trust that she would come through on other agreements that could have negatively impacted my business, especially after money was involved.

Expectations

Expectations are either realistic or unrealistic. Realistic expectations account for what is and allow for you to flow with reality, whether you like it or not. I do get it...reality can be unpleasant and uncomfortable at times. Still, reality offers the best chance to make good decisions. Unrealistic expectations, on the other hand, are about what you hope for or fantasize about or think what "should" be, anything except reality. And because unrealistic expectations are not aligned with reality, they set you and other people up to fail. Reality supersedes unrealistic expectations.

> Fiancés Julia and Wyatt provide an example of realistic expectations. They had uncomfortable conversations about money and lifestyle while dating. Instead of *hoping* that love would be enough to make things work out, Julia and Wyatt consciously prepared for marriage by clarifying their expected roles. They agreed that Julia would manage their money because she was better with finances and that Wyatt would manage their vacations and social calendar because he was a good organizer. Ten years later, their relationship continues to flow well because of their realistic expectations and because each fulfills their agreed upon roles.

One very important differentiation between realistic and unrealistic expectations is about patterns.

For example, Kayla's sister Dena asked to borrow $200 to buy supplies for her newborn. Kayla said yes with the agreement that her sister would pay her back in a month, and then she gave Dena her debit card information. A few days later, Kayla's bank notified her about potential fraudulent activity that totaled $1000. Kayla was livid over her sister's betrayal—spending more than they agreed. However, Kayla realized in therapy that her expectation that Dena would keep her word was unrealistic because Dena had the pattern of broken agreements with family, including Kayla previously. Family members had even declined loaning Dena money before she asked Kayla. While she *hoped* Dena would keep this agreement because it involved a baby, Kayla's expectation that her sister would was unrealistic and compromised her financially.

3.2 Activity: Your Mental Boundary

Who in your life consistently keeps their word or communicates why they can't?

_____

Who doesn't keep their word?

_____

Is your expectation of him/her/them realistic or hopeful?

_____

3. Emotional Boundary

The emotional boundary is the least clear because there is no obvious line of separation between individuals, as there is with the physical and your body or with the mental and agreements. Because of this blurred line, the emotional boundary is closely tied to the individuation function of boundaries.

As mentioned in chapter 2, individuation is a normal human process through which each of us gains a more clear understanding of who we are independently and who we are in relation to others, which usually occurs during the teenage years. This clarity enables you to become your unique self and develop your inherent talents and gifts to share with the world. Without proper individuation, you may experience low self-confidence/esteem/worth, seek unhealthy love and/or approval from others, become enmeshed, and become vulnerable to abusers.

Understanding Enmeshment & Entanglement

Simply put, enmeshment is basically emotional and identity confusion when one or both people in a relationship lack individual sense of self. Enmeshment occurs in all types of relationships— marriage, siblings, parent-child, friends, coworkers, teacher-student, business partners, etc. Lack of clarity about who you are puts you at risk for having poor emotional boundaries, which can lead to being manipulated, mistreated, abused, codependent, controlled, and victimized in other ways. Your human uniqueness becomes entangled and bound up with another person's unhealthiness.

According to Scott M. Stanley Ph.D., enmeshment *"implies the obliteration of one or both identities in some manner."*

On the other hand, Dr. Stanley posits that we-ness is a healthy, thriving, and safe relationship between two separate individuals, each having a clear sense of self. Another crucial difference between we-ness and enmeshment is that those in a healthy relationship have shared goals. With enmeshment the most dominant of the duo imposes their will upon the other, almost absorbing the less dominant one's personality…hence the *obliteration.*

Below are two (of many) ways to view enmeshment. Be aware that the solid circles do not indicate perfection or completeness. The solid lines merely represent separate individuals and the rigid nature of their boundaries.

Diagram 3.0 depicts two people in a relationship who perceive themselves as *missing something*—defective, weak, and unworthy. Their faulty self-image creates poor emotional boundaries which leads each of them to an unhealthy need for approval and enmeshment (the overlapping circles).

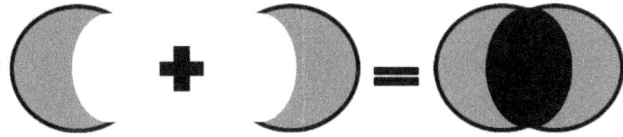

Diagram 3.1 illustrates two people in a relationship where enmeshment involves the more dominant person overriding the less dominant person. And the less dominant person attempts to also become what the dominant one wants, even if it goes against their own beliefs and values, which is a spiritual boundary issue and is discussed below.

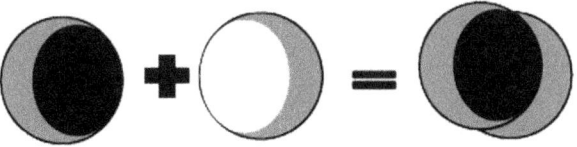

For more clarity, Diagram 3.2 depicts a healthy relationship between two people. Each person has a good understanding of who they are, including their thoughts, emotions, choices, strengths, areas for improvement, and innate gifts. Basically, each individual's boundaries are intact with spaces to adjust to context. And they come together in wholeness, rather than emptiness and voids to fill.

Being unclear where you begin and end and where another person begins and ends is a poor boundary that presents as the control issues described in the examples that follow:

Taking on someone else's stuff

In this presentation of a poor emotional boundary, the goal is to control the outcomes for another person. The one with the poor boundary is convinced that it's their noble responsibility to protect loved ones and others they feel sorry for from the negative consequences of their choices. Think of the parent who oversees and negatively criticizes their adult child's choice of partner or career or expenditures to make them a better adult, even though the adult child works and maintains his own home.

> Josie gets really angry when her 29 year old son buys a new video game or spends money hanging out with his friends after he pays his bills. She repeatedly criticizes him for being irresponsible and for not saving more money. Josie's excessive criticism is her attempt to control her son's money and his choices.

Seeking someone to take on your stuff

This presentation of a poor emotional boundary is about drawing others in to take control of and responsibility for your life. You entice others to rescue you with your woeful stories of how things just don't work out for you such as *'nobody likes me'* or *'I can't catch a break'*. Think of the person who told you their life story after just meeting you. Oversharing is a common expression of an emotional boundary issue.

> In college, I went on a dinner date with a professional young man who was handsome and who presented himself well. At dinner, however, most of what he talked about was his ex-girlfriend. He complained about what she did not do for him sexually and otherwise. This was not the conversation for a first date, although the intention of his oversharing was to entice me to *do better* than his ex-girlfriend did to make him happy. I wasn't interested in rescuing him nor trying to please him in an attempt to make up for his self-described negative experiences with his ex-girlfriend. When he called after the date, I declined to see him again and explained why.

3.3 Activity: Your Emotional Boundaries

1. Who do you try to rescue from bad things, the negative consequences of their choices?

_____

2. Are you successful at saving him/her/them?   □ Yes   □ No

3. Do you feel capable of handling your own life?   □ Yes   □ No

4. If no, then who takes charge of your narrative?

_____

4. Spiritual Boundary

The Spiritual Boundary is not about religion for me. It's about connection. How well connected are you to your true self, to your loved ones, to your community, to your creator? Please note that how authentically connected you are to yourself enables you to connect authentically with others. The Spiritual Boundary is also about how well aligned your principles and values are with your choices. When you are well connected to your true, innate self and when your choices reflect your beliefs and values, you flow with reality much more easily. When you aren't connected to self or aligned, then an internal war is born, which often leads to anxiety and depression.

Dwayne loves to travel and is open to getting to know people from different backgrounds. His current boyfriend made him feel like a god with gifts, promises, and compliments when they began dating. Yet, the boyfriend doesn't like to go far from home and he frowns upon Dwayne socializing with people he doesn't approve of. So, Dwayne stopped traveling and interacting with family members and friends who his boyfriend doesn't like. He is experiencing depression because he feels stuck between doing what brings him joy (traveling and socializing) and doing what his boyfriend wants.

Leona has been a casino dealer for 10 years. She was excited about the job in the beginning because it paid very well, enabling her to pay off debt and establish a comfortable lifestyle. As the years passed, Leona grew increasingly agitated at work and overindulged in drinking alcohol and partying. Witnessing people lose their life savings and the heartache that came with gambling was depressing to her. While Leona understood that the gambling adults were responsible for their own choices, she realized in therapy that dealing casino games did not align with her values. Leona believed that gambling was harmful and wrong. And in order to justify and mask her participation in games of chance, she turned to alcohol and carousing.

3.4 Activity: Your Spiritual Boundary

1. Who in your life supports what brings you joy?

_____

2. Do you ignore what you need to please someone else?
□ Yes   □ No

3. Do you make choices that go against your values?
□ Yes   □ No

SUMMARY

Understanding the different types of boundaries is important in protecting and nurturing yourself.

Being able to recognize the specific boundary involved in different situations enables you to more quickly identify the most pertinent issues you face and to make the best decisions available to protect and nurture yourself. Actions to take to protect and nurture yourself with the different boundary types include:

Physical boundary – moving or removing your body.

Mental boundary – reevaluating your agreements and expectations, making adjustments as needed.

Emotional boundary – discerning and separating your issues from those of another person.

Spiritual boundary – connecting with self and aligning your choices with your principles and values.

CHAPTER 4

DRAWING YOUR LINE IN THE SAND

"'Setting a boundary' means protecting your joy and well-being by telling someone to stop a harmful behavior."
—Lauren Martin, Anger is a Storm

The foundation of healthy boundaries is laid by your line in the sand. This line represents how far you will go, how far you will allow others to take you, and how much you allow them to take from you. Boundaries are the line where what you will and will not tolerate meet. Think back to your childhood. Remember drawing a line in the grass or on the ground with a stick or your toe? You dared your playmate to cross it with pursed lips which conveyed how serious you were about that line, the proverbial line in the sand. *"Cross this line and..."* The child in you intuitively knew that you have boundaries, that some things were acceptable to you, and more importantly some not.

You also knew, intuitively, that the crossing of your line yielded consequences. *"Don't cross this line or else..."* The 'or else' communicated the consequences you would have applied if and when your line had gotten crossed. There were consequences if your playmate broke the plane of your line. Perhaps you stopped speaking to him. Maybe you didn't share your candy with her. Or you didn't include them in play time with other kids. In either case, you as a child recognized that you have boundaries and boundary violations have consequences.

The purpose of such consequences is to teach others where your line is and how to respect it. This remains true in adulthood, even though boundaries look more sophisticated and complex. Still, healthy boundaries are your line in the sand where what you will and won't tolerate meet. And to be the effective teaching tool that boundaries are designed to be, violations require negative consequences for those who violate them to dissuade them from doing it again.

For the record, healthy boundaries necessitate reinforcement with positive consequences. Reinforcing appropriate behavior increases the likelihood that it will recur. Consequences will be discussed further in Chapter 13--Affirming Your Boundaries.

It is, however, nearly impossible to apply consequences when your boundaries are crossed if you are not clear about what your line in the sand signifies. Are you okay with being disrespected? Do you tolerate abuse or mistreatment? Is anyone able to control or take your time, energy, money?

Without a clear understanding of where your line in the sand is, the foundation of your boundaries will be deficient, leaving you vulnerable to undue influences that can lead to physical, mental, emotional, and/or spiritual harm.

Thus, you must identify for yourself what and where your line in the sand is in every area of your life. Note here that boundaries are contextual. They vary depending on who is involved, when and where the situation occurs, which of your boundaries apply, and for how long this situation lasts. The contextual nature of boundaries will be discussed further in Chapter 10--Living in Context with Your Boundaries.

> Regina was angry about how a friend spoke to her in front of others. So we talked about boundaries. Regina immediately asked, *"How do you set boundaries?"* I answered her question with a question: *Why do you want to set boundaries?* She went silent. So I followed up with another question: *What boundaries do you want to set?* Regina

remained silent, still confused by my questions because she hadn't considered *what* boundaries to set nor even *why* set them.

How is irrelevant without *why* and *what*. Far too often, people seek the 'how-to' and without any understanding of or clarity about their intentions nor the specific results they want to achieve. You can search for anything online these days. Such searches include how to lose weight, how to meditate, how to sleep well, and how to set boundaries. Yet, many of my clients (and people I know personally) do not implement nor commit to the how either because they don't have the *what* they want exactly or because they are not clear about the goal they strive for, in my opinion. So start with your why to lay the foundation for what you want and to provide your purpose for the *how*, which will enable you to endure distractions from and persevere through any challenges you may encounter in pursuit of your goals. So, let's start with *why*.

4.1 Activity: What is your purpose for setting boundaries?

_____

_____

Identifying Your Deal Breakers

Once you are clear on *why* to set boundaries, you can identify what your boundaries are. This is where you decide what you will and will not tolerate, including your deal breakers. These are behaviors that you will absolutely not tolerate. Deal breakers are such egregious and harmful actions that are unforgivable to you. What actions of others will end your relationship or significantly alter your connection and contact with them?

An example of a deal breaker comes from the movie Embattled starring Stephen Dorff. His character Cash was married to Jade. When Cash struggled with his career, he became physically aggressive with Jade. As she was leaving him, he apologized and begged her to stay. Jade reminded him of the agreement they made when they married.

Cash: *I'll be back Sunday morning. Will you still be here? ...come on Jade.*

Jade: *Cash, I warned you before we got married. Zero tolerance. We had a contract.*

Cash: *I know. I'm sorry baby.*

Jade: *Me too.*

Jade kept her part of the agreement and left the marriage.

Keep in mind that your deal breakers are commitments to yourself. So make sure that they are ones you are ready to follow through with, as Jade did. Deal breakers are not threats. They are not leverage for you to coerce or manipulate the other person into doing what you want. And they are not 'maybes'. Deal breakers are your non-negotiable requirements to remain in a relationship with someone. You can compromise on who washes dishes or changes the baby's diaper or even who is head of household. Yet, your deal breakers are not up for debate nor negotiation. A deal breaker is *'If this happens, then I will end this relationship'*.

Examples of what unhealthy boundaries look like are presented later in Chapter 6--Revealing Emotional Boundary Red Flags, Chapter 7—Seeing Physical, Mental, and Spiritual Red Flags, and Chapter 13—Affirming Your Boundaries. For now, allow your intuition to inform you of your top 3-5 deal breakers that cross your line of tolerance and represent the end of a relationship.

The purpose of this activity is not about judging or grading you. So please don't filter or search your mind for the *right* answer. Just write and list your deal breakers as they occur to you now.

4.2 Activity: List Your Deal Breakers

1. _____

2. _____

3. _____

4. _____

5. _____

Being aware that your line in the sand, where what you will and will not tolerate meet, enables you to recognize boundary issues in real time or in such a way that you realize the need to affirm your boundaries. Then understanding of the need for appropriate consequences will become more clear to you and more natural to implement.

SUMMARY

There are layers above setting boundaries. These layers are about understanding what boundaries are, their purpose, and being clear about your line in the sand—the line where what you will and will not tolerate meet, which includes your deal breakers. Your understanding is the foundation upon which you strengthen your boundaries.

SECTION II:

LIVING YOUR BOUNDARIES

CHAPTER 5

RECOGNIZING YOUR HEALTHY BOUNDARIES

*"Boundaries are like healthy roots; they ground you
and let you thrive."*
—Unknown

How will you know when your boundaries have been violated? Let's begin with what healthy boundaries actually look like. As an ongoing process, boundaries go much deeper than just saying "no". In truth, boundaries are more about not putting yourself in the position of having to say *yes* or having to say *no*. Finding yourself in that position means that you did not adequately guard yourself beforehand.

On the other hand, wearing your boundaries like a second skin enables you to navigate your life in such a way that produces the most rewarding and joyful experiences available to you. To that end, knowing what healthy, unhealthy, and violations of boundaries look like in real time is key. The examples below provide the seeds of the intellectual understanding of how healthy boundaries present.

KNOWING HEALTHY BOUNDARIES

Boundaries that respect and support the integrity of your humanity and who you are individually are healthy. Your best interest on the physical, mental, emotional, and spiritual levels is affirmed in your interactions with others, even if they don't get what they want from you and even if you disagree with them. For clear visuals, see the list with examples below. Note that this list is not exhaustive and you may already be aware of other presentations of your healthy boundaries.

You can think of healthy boundaries as green flags, as indicators of what's working and what to repeat.

1. Accepting "No"

Anyone who respects you will accept your "no" even if they don't like being told so, because they understand that no one gets their way all the time and that you have the right to choose what is in your best interest.

> Genny and Kate worked together for a few years and became good friends. When Genny received a job offer in another state that was within driving distance, she and Kate made an agreement to alternate visiting each other every month. Their plan worked for a few months until Genny's difficulty adjusting to her new circumstances took its toll on her. The stress of moving, the increased cost of living, and the limited social circle were depressing to her. And when Genny's turn to visit arrived, she called Kate to tell her that she was too depressed to make the 2 hour drive. Kate thought of the plans they made, sighed deeply, then said to Genny, *"I'm sorry you're not feeling well. I understand if you need to skip this month's visit. Do you want to talk about it? Is there anything I can do to help?"*

Unhealthy boundary presentations include the following examples:

❖ Kate getting angry and belittling Genny with statements like '*you're so selfish'*.
❖ Genny ignoring her own needs and pleasing Kate by going anyway, triggering anxiety while driving and worsening her depression.

2. Disagreeing with Grace

Anyone who respects you will not attack you personally or get mean when you disagree with them, as happened during the pandemic when friends attacked each other for diverse opinions, which ended many of those relationships.

> Jake and Dwayne agreed on many topics. Worship was not one of them. Jake believed that attending church and hearing sermons were the proper ways to worship. Dwayne, on the other hand, believed that worship was not confined to a building and that expressing his reverence daily was suitable. During their first heated debate about the right way to express devotion, both made valid points. Instead of continuing the circular attempts to prove who was right, Jake stopped and said, *"Hey man, we clearly don't see eye to eye. So let's agree to disagree."* Dwayne agreed to that and their friendship remained on respectful terms.

Unhealthy boundary presentations include the following examples:

- ❖ Either one of them threatening the other with damnation.
- ❖ Attacking each other personally with name-calling or put-downs.
- ❖ Ending their friendship abruptly and stop speaking.

3. Taking Responsibility for Your Own Happiness

You take responsibility for your own happiness by protecting and nurturing yourself. While those in your life can support your highest good, you don't wait nor hope for others to guess what you want or need and give it to you automatically.

> Meranda was recently divorced. Being on her own for the first time in 20 years unnerved her and triggered anxiety about being alone and not having someone, her husband, make decisions for her. So she went on dates with men whom

she didn't find attractive only to avoid her loneliness and her fear of making decisions for herself. However, the unfulfilling dates exhausted Meranda. During another uncomfortable date, she realized that she was wasting time on these meaningless encounters and decided to develop a healthier relationship with herself. So, the next day Meranda started therapy to help her grieve the loss of her marriage, to heal, and to develop self-confidence.

Unhealthy boundary presentations include the following examples:

❖ Meranda continues to date, looking for the man who would rescue her from her fears and her responsibilities for herself.
❖ Meranda commits to the first man who promised to take care of her to avoid her fears.

4. You understand that consequences are required

You get that setting and affirming boundaries requires appropriate consequences because human nature is such that individuals will continue to do what they can get away with—Boundary Truth #1 from Chapter 9 – Understanding the Truths About Boundaries. So accordingly, you identify and apply positive consequences for those who respect your boundaries and apply negative consequences for those who don't.

I had a client who initiated therapy to process the traumas he experienced growing up in an abusive home so he didn't pass them on to his own children. During the intake session I explained the scheduling policy to him, as I do all clients. The policy limits the number of no-shows and late cancellations that clients can have because attending scheduled sessions is the first level of commitments required for clients to achieve the healing they seek. If they don't show up, then they can't learn and do the necessary work. Also, missing therapy meetings inhibits growth and progress because as time passes between sessions, old habits resume. He seemed sincere and agreed to the policy.

This client no-showed for his 3rd session, which was not due to an emergency. I reminded him of the appointment policy. He acknowledged it and agreed again to cancel at least 24 hours in advance when necessary. Then he no-showed for his 5th session because he scheduled his appointment during his work hours. Again, I reminded him about the policy and informed him that if he missed again, then he would be discharged from my client caseload. This client agreed again to abide by the policy and volunteered that he would be more mindful when scheduling appointments with me.

The following week, this client no-showed again – 3 times in 6 sessions. He later messaged me that he was driving during the appointment time. As much as I wanted to work with this client on his healing journey, I realized that not enforcing the scheduling policy that he agreed to multiple times would enable his betrayals of the agreements he made, lead to more no-shows, and impede his healing process. So, I discharged him.

Unhealthy boundary presentations include the following examples:

- ❖ I felt sorry for this client, continued to schedule him and tolerate his no-shows, which would have frustrated me because the missed sessions wasted time, resulted in loss of income for me, and eliminated the possibility of filling the slot with a committed client.
- ❖ I punished the client for missing sessions with a negative attitude and reprimanded when he did show up.

Chapter 13, Affirming Your Boundaries is all about consequences for boundary violations, how to communicate and apply them, and provides more information and examples.

5. Being present and attuned to your intuition

When you are present, you can see both healthy and unhealthy boundaries in real time. The present moment is the time when you receive information from your intuition, which communicates with you about potential problems and safety issues. Mindlessness, being unaware of what is happening within and around you because you're fretting about the future or dwelling on the past, closes you off from your innate intelligence and your personal protection. Healthy boundaries enable you to be present as often as possible.

Julie was on a lunch date on a Saturday afternoon with a man she recently met. She was not very impressed by him, largely due to them not having any interests in common. When the conversation turned to work, he piqued her interest by telling her that his company was hiring because she had been job hunting. Seeing her excitement, he offered to show her around the company where he worked. Julie took him up on the offer and she followed him in her own car.

During the drive, Julie felt a pit in her stomach and a sinking feeling in her heart. She recognized those sensations as signs from her intuition. Then Julie said to herself, *why am I going to this man's job when it's closed and no one else would be there? This isn't a good idea.* Julie stopped following him and went home. Her uncomfortable physical sensations then ceased. Julie later learned that this man was on the National Sex Offender Registry. She thanked her intuition.

> *"Intuition is perception beyond the physical senses that is meant to assist you."*
> —Gary Zukav

SUMMARY

Signs of healthy boundaries are green flags, which inform you about what is working and what to repeat. Green flags are the opposite of red flags. Think of it like a stop light – red means to stop and green signifies when to go.

5.1 Activity: Below is a short list of self-care and self-advocacy actions that represent more indicators of healthy boundaries. Check the actions you currently engage in.

- □ Trust your intuition
- □ Positive self-talk
- □ Surround yourself with nurturing and encouraging people
- □ Limit negative people in your life
- □ Engage in enriching activities
- □ Minimize distractions from your well-being
- □ Set realistic goals
- □ Speak up when appropriate
- □ Be yourself
- □ Prioritize your health: sleep, nutrition, activities

5.2 Activity: Your Healthy Boundary

Share a situation you experienced that reflects one of the 5 healthy boundary examples above:

_____

_____

_____

_____

RECOGNIZING UNHEALTHY BOUNDARIES INTRODUCTION

"Whatever you are willing to put up with is exactly what you will get."
—Unknown

Unlike healthy boundaries, unhealthy boundaries involve attacks intended to break down your integrity, disrespect your person, and diminish your thoughts, feelings, emotions, sexuality, finances, and spirituality. In order to get their way, the violator uses tactics like belittling your opinion, unconstructive or excessive criticism, telling you that you're unlovable or ugly or unwanted, and punishing you for not giving them whatever it is they want. Typically, the person violating your boundaries is only interested in what they desire and what they can get from you, and not what your highest good is.

Allow me to introduce the concept of unhealthy boundaries being either too open or too closed. Boundaries that are too open attract abusive and harmful people who seek to get what they want in the quickest and easiest way possible. On the other hand, boundaries that are too closed are more like walls that block authentic love and connection from entering that person's inner circle. These walls also prohibit the person from sharing and expressing authentic love and connection.

Red flags are boundary violations in action that are based upon a person's boundaries being too open or too closed. While familiarizing yourself with the concepts of boundaries, being able to see red flags in real time is crucial to protecting and nurturing yourself as soon as possible. Seeing red flags as you experience them is empowering because you then have the opportunity to act in your healthiest interest on the spot or shortly thereafter to minimize or shield yourself from the harm you face.

As I wrote about the chapter about red flags, I realized that the majority of the examples are emotional boundary issues. This surprised me. And I was led to separate the real-life red flag examples by the type of boundary involved. Thus this chapter, Revealing Emotional Boundary Red Flags, addresses emotional boundary issues. As a reminder, the emotional boundary is about trying to control another person, control their outcomes, or to enlist someone to rescue or save you. The following chapter, Seeing Physical, Mental, and Spiritual Red Flags, shares red flag examples for physical, mental, and spiritual boundaries.

Also keep in mind that boundary issues can overlap in the type of boundary involved. For the purposes of this book, the examples of red flags are separated by the type of boundary involved to enhance your understanding.

CHAPTER 6

REVEALING EMOTIONAL BOUNDARY RED FLAGS

"If you ignore the red flags, embrace the heartache to come."
—Amanda Mosher

Emotional Boundaries are the most difficult to discern because they are not tangible or concrete like physical boundaries. Nor are they as clear cut as agreements in mental boundaries or values in spiritual boundaries. Yet, emotional boundaries violations are abundant and often set the stage for issues with the physical, mental, and spiritual boundaries.

Below are just a few examples of how unhealthy emotional boundaries manifest in real life. This list lays the foundation for you to be able see these red flags in real time. Keep in mind that the following red flags occur long before your deal breakers in Chapter 4 – Drawing Your Line in the Sand.

1. Undermining Self-confidence

Chipping away at the self-esteem of another person has the goal of undermining their self-confidence. The goal's purpose is for you, your spouse or partner, a family member, or friend to position themselves as the primary or sole source of validation for the person you are criticizing, which gives control over that person.

Sheila was excited about a nice, handsome, professional man with money wanting to date her. She felt special until their

3rd date when he nicely asked her, "Are you really going to wear *those* shoes with that dress?

Poor boundary:

> - Sheila asks him what should she wear to show she cares about his opinion.
> - Sheila changes to please him to make a good impression.

Healthy boundary:

> - ✓ Sheila responds, "Yes, I am." Or "They match nicely with my dress."
> - ✓ Sheila wears what she is comfortable wearing.

2. Belittling

Name-calling, assassinating your character, demonizing your behavior, and put-downs are forms of belittling that you, your spouse or partner, a family member, or friend use against someone else when they don't obey or conform to the demands of others.

Kara decided years ago to stop loaning money to family and friends because of broken agreements. And she has clearly communicated her policy to them. When Kara's cousin Diane asks to borrow $500, she says "no". Even though Diane was aware of Kara's policy, she then turns left and says, *"What, the big wig is too good to help the little people now?"*

Poor boundary:

> - Kara gives in so Diane won't be angry and loans her the money.
> - Kara feels guilty for keeping her agreement with herself and declining to loan Diane the money.

Healthy boundary:

- ✓ Kara respectfully reminds Diane about her policy and declines to make the loan.
- ✓ Kara doesn't engage Diane's negative criticism.

3. Emotional Blackmail

You, your spouse or partner, a family member, or friend pulls the *If you love me, then you would…* This tactic manipulates the other person into giving in to your demands by guilt-tripping him/her/them.

One of my high school classmates, Angela, was so excited about going out with Jerry because she had a crush on him since junior high. After one month of hanging out, Jerry began asking for sex. Each time, she told him that she wasn't ready. Jerry finally said to Angela, *"If you love me then you'll show me."*

Poor boundary:

- ➢ Angela gives in and has sex with Jerry even though she did not want to.
- ➢ Angela berates herself for being immature and not woman enough to please her Jerry.

Healthy boundary:

- ✓ Angela tells Jerry that she loves him and is not ready to have sex.
- ✓ Angela stays true to herself and accepts if he breaks up with her.

4. Open Book

You, your spouse or partner, a family member, or friend are an "open book". This means that you quickly, easily, and inappropriately share your personal information. Have you ever met someone and knew far too much about them in the first few minutes of meeting? One purpose of oversharing is to invite the other person to rescue and take care of you. Recall the example of the young man I had a date with in college in chapter 3. He spent the majority of the date complaining about what his ex-girlfriend did not do for him, attempting to entice me to try and do better than she did. It did not work, as I wasn't and still am not interested in rescuing adults from the consequences of their choices.

Sabrina was in therapy because her relationships didn't last. This was true for romantic interests and friendships. Romantically, Sabrina shared with her new love interest the history of her failed relationships, what she did wrong, and what she wants to do better within the first few dates. Her relationships were fast and furious, ending as quickly as they started.

Poor boundary:

➤ Sabrina does not hold back and tells the romantic interest all about herself in order to draw that person in to rescuing her.

Healthy boundary:

✓ Sabrina holds back sharing intimate details about herself until she discerns if the romantic interest is a good fit for her.
✓ Sabrina allows the relationship to unfold naturally without forcing it.

Another purpose of oversharing is to be the one in the know, to gossip. Anyone who is inappropriate with their own business tends to be irresponsible with that of other people. Those who overshare are eager to tell on themselves and others.

I had a friend who was very at ease about sharing her personal information with others, including her age. I was not. My friend, Tamara, asked me why I didn't talk my age because I should be proud of it. I told her that I've always been a private person, I'm uncomfortable disclosing too much about myself, and that I only share myself with those in my inner circle. Tamara said she understood. Then at a later date during a casual conversation with associates at a social event, Tamara blurted out, "Oh Glen, you're x years old so I'm sure you remember that time." I was angered by Tamara's betrayal.

Poor boundary:

> ➤ Because Tamara openly and easily shares about herself to most people in many situations, she tells my age without my consent.
> ➤ Tamara shared my age knowing that I was private about it.

Healthy boundary

> ✓ Tamara does not share my age without my knowledge or consent.
> ✓ I remind Tamara not to share my private information.

5. Blaming Others

Someone who does not take responsibility for the consequences of their choices and consistently blames others is exhibiting an emotional boundary red flag. The reality is that each of us humans will yield a positive, negative, or neutral consequence to each choice that we make and each act we perform. Those unwilling to acknowledge or accept this fact of the Human Condition will also blame you for their harmful choices and failures.

Melvin met another parent at their sons' basketball game and thought he'd be cool to hang out with. After sitting with Bryan for 2 games, Melvin decided to not pursue a friendship because Bryan complained often about how his ex-wife ruined their marriage, how his boss made it hard to do his job, and how he just couldn't get a break in life because people sabotaged him.

Poor boundary:

- ➤ Melvin chimes in and agrees with Bryan that he gets shafted a lot.
- ➤ Melvin excuses Bryan's blame and accusations in those situations.

Healthy boundary:

- ✓ Melvin respectfully distances himself from Bryan.
- ✓ Melvin doesn't engage in long or intense conversations with Bryan.
- ✓ Melvin changes the subject when Bryan blames others for his mistakes.

In the anger management groups for male batterers that I co-facilitated, all of the batterers blamed their female partners for the violence they themselves inflicted – *"She made me mad"*, *"She should've kept her mouth shut"*, *"If she didn't…, then I wouldn't have"*.

Poor boundary:

- ➤ The batterer blames the victim for his choice to be violent.
- ➤ The batterer chooses to be violent rather than manage his own emotions and behavior.

Healthy boundary:

- ✓ The batterer acknowledges and accepts responsibility for his emotions and reactions.
- ✓ The batterer chooses to engage in emotional intelligence to manage his anger.
- ✓ The batterer calms himself then converses with his partner about what's bothering him.
- ✓ The batterer seeks help to learn how to manage his emotions and behavior better.

6. Withholding and punishment

Mary goes completely silent for hours when her new partner Sarina disagrees with her about things. Mary wants to solely decide how much they spend on entertainment, where they go for dinner, and whose family to visit for the holidays. Sarina believes she should have a say because they're in the relationship together. Yet, when she voices her opinion Mary gives her the cold shoulder.

Poor boundary:

- ➢ Sarina beats herself up for speaking up and causing Mary to stop speaking to her.
- ➢ Sarina berates herself for disagreeing with Mary.
- ➢ Sarina stops sharing her wants and needs with Mary.

Healthy boundary:

- ✓ Sarina speaks with Mary when both are calm and not distracted about making decisions together.
- ✓ Sarina expresses herself and self-advocates authentically.
- ✓ Sarina reflects on her choices if Mary continues to punish her for disagreeing and for speaking up.

7. Taking on someone else's stuff

Integrating someone else's behavior and emotions as your own, is an emotional boundary issue in the form of enmeshment where you are not clear where you begin and end and where the other person begins and ends. Recall the discussion and diagrams from Chapter 3 – Categorizing Your Boundaries.

> Bridgette is angry with her husband, Joseph, because of an argument they had about her spending too much money. Bridgette complains to her sister Amelia about the argument. At the next family get-together, Amelia completely ignores Joseph because of what her sister told her. Amelia acted out Bridgette's anger toward Joseph as if it was her own, even though Joseph was not inappropriate with nor disrespectful of Amelia.

Poor boundary:

- ➢ Amelia takes on Bridgette's anger and gets angry with Joseph.
- ➢ Amelia acts out Bridgette's anger by ignoring Joseph.

Healthy boundary:

- ✓ Amelia empathizes with Bridgette and offers her support.
- ✓ Amelia behaves appropriately with Joseph.

8. Quick commitment pressure

Pressuring someone for a commitment is an urgency to "seal the deal" quickly, robbing the targeted person the time and space needed to adequately evaluate their choices. Think of the stereotypical used car dealer. The salesman's forcefulness in telling the customer why they should buy that car right now is called a "hard sell". Of course, this pressure is presented as completely beneficial to the buyer who would miss out on something awesome if they don't make the purchase at that time. And if the target doesn't make the quick commitment, then the one applying the pressure belittles and insults the target. The same is true in other types of relationships.

I met a woman through a mutual friend. This woman wanted to establish a friendship with me quickly. At the time, I worked 6 days per week and didn't have a lot of time for new, casual associations, plus my intuition alerted me to be aware of her. While she presented as nice, she seemed desperate for attention. So shortly after meeting, I declined her multiple invitations to have coffee, lunch, dinner, and a drink. She then commented, *"You're a hard nut to crack"*. I replied with *"I'm not a project; I'm a busy person."* She stopped demanding my attention.

Poor boundary:

> ➢ I ignore my intuition and make time to spend with her.
> ➢ I interpret her neediness as she just really wants a friendship with me and give in.
> ➢ I people please and give in to her "niceness".

Healthy boundary:

> ✓ I heed my intuition and keep my distance.

In another example, Regina was in a good place. She was promoted at work with a salary increase that enabled her to afford her own home, she had a supportive circle of family and friends, and she looked forward to finishing holiday crafts. At a friend's social event, Regina met Vanessa. They learned that they have a lot in common and hit it off. Vanessa took Regina to dinner the following week where she expressed her attraction to Regina and desire for a romantic relationship. Flattered, Regina blushed then went on to say that she was not interested in a committed, full-time relationship. Vanessa said she understood and agreed to just be friends. Over the next few weeks, Vanessa called Regina several times per day to say *"I'm just thinking about you"*. *"Just wondering how you're doing"*. *"Wish we could spend more time together"*. *"I miss you."* Regina found herself answering Vanessa's calls and responding to her every message even though she still wanted to be solo.

Poor boundary:

> ➢ Vanessa pressures Regina to be in a relationship with her excessive attention.
> ➢ Vanessa ignores Regina's relationship boundary and pursues her anyway.
> ➢ Regina defies her desire for a casual relationship and behaves as if she is in a committed, full-time relationship with Vanessa.

Healthy boundary:

> ✓ Regina resists Vanessa's love bombing and does not establish a romantic relationship with her.
> ✓ Regina stops communicating with Vanessa.
> ✓ Vanessa respects Regina's desires and remains friends.

9. You expect others to "know" and fulfill your needs automatically

This unhealthy emotional boundary is about someone else rescuing and saving you from your life, your choices, and responsibility for yourself without you having to communicate what you want or need from them. So you get angry, sad, or disappointed when someone doesn't guess what you want because you believe that he/she/they should know what you think, need, feel, and want and provide it automatically.

Dan is retired and babysits his 4 year old grandson Monday-Friday so his daughter, a single parent, can save money on childcare. One of Dan's college classmates invited him to an annual reunion luncheon on Wednesday. When Dan told his daughter about the luncheon, he expected her to say something like 'that's great dad. I'll find someone else to babysit that day.' She didn't. So Dan grew angry because she should've known that he wanted to attend the event and offered to give him the day off.

"How dare she? I save her a lot of money and she can't give me one day off? So ungrateful!" Dan did not ask for nor declare what he wanted and his anger led him to be curt with his daughter.

Poor boundary:

> ➤ Dan assumes and hopes that his daughter will read his mind and then give him the day off like he wants.
> ➤ Dan gets angry with his daughter and is curt with her.
> ➤ Dan does not self-advocate to get his needs met.

Healthy boundary:

> ✓ Dan tells his daughter that he wants to attend the luncheon.
> ✓ Dan asks his daughter to find someone else to babysit on Wednesday.
> ✓ Dan offers to help his daughter find a substitute babysitter.

10. Violence

You, your family, friend, mate, or coworker threatens another person with anger or violence, is abusive physically, mentally, emotionally, and/or spiritually to get your/their way. Some examples of violence involve slapping, punching, kicking, pushing, pinching, blocking the path or door, threats to harm, and holding on to someone physically. This red flag is about overt control, which is the purpose of the violence. Typically, the overt control is subtle in the beginning of relationships then escalates over time.

Abuse:

The abuse aspect of this violence red flag is about manipulation and control, and involves threats to harm you, threats to leave you, name-calling, saying no one else would want you, discounting your experience with saying something similar to "you didn't really…". Abuse also includes pressure to have sex, do drugs, drink alcohol or conform, isolating you from family and friends, taking your money and other resources, plus more.

Coercion:

This red flag is also about manipulation and involves emotional blackmail, guilt-tripping, relentless *encouragement* to comply. Coercion obligates the person being manipulated into paying back the abuser's fake generosity. One example is *I don't usually do that but I'll do it for you.*

> One Thanksgiving, a batterer punched his wife in the face in front of family members who did not intervene. The next year, he didn't like the dinner plan she wanted and raised up on her as if to punch her again to get her to back down and do things his way. The coercion worked because of his previous abuse. His gesture alone was enough to trigger in her the fear that he would hit her again, so she acquiesced to what he wanted.

Poor boundary:

> ➤ The batterer punches his wife to impose his will.

> ➢ The batterer threatens his wife with his body language to get his way.
> ➢ The wife stays with the batterer after he punches her.
> ➢ The wife blames herself for making her husband hit her.

Healthy boundary:

> ✓ The batterer effectively self-regulates and doesn't abuse his wife.
> ✓ The batterer respects his wife's dinner plan and opinions.
> ✓ The batterer receives treatment for his abusive behavior.
> ✓ The wife leaves the batterer after he punches her.

11. Excessive attention

Excessive attention involves being overly attentive with affection, compliments, terms of endearment, gifts, and just appearing to deeply care about 'the special person'. Some people call this love-bombing because it is an explosion of adoration. This excessive attention is an unsustainable, fraudulent manipulation designed to make the target feel special, needed, and the only one able to make the stalker happy. Yes, the flip side of appearing to love is stalking. Once hooked, however, the love-bomber stops the acts of affection and their controlling nature is revealed.

Rinaldo was very excited to see Gail again. It had been a few years since they spoke. This encounter occurred at an event to celebrate a mutual friend of theirs. Gail and Rinaldo exchanged the usual niceties—*How are you? How have you been?* Not long after reminiscing about their mutual loved one, Rinaldo turned on the charm.

I really missed you. I think about you all the time. I love you.

Gail took a deep breath, looked Rinaldo in his eyes, and responded that they were there to celebrate their friend, not to hook up.

I know. I'm sorry. You're so beautiful, I just can't help myself from loving you.

She reminded him that they never dated and she still was not interested in a romantic relationship with him. Gail added, *"Please stop talking to me like that."*

Okay. I understand. Rinaldo still continued the love bombing via text for a few days after the event anyway.

Gail responded, *"This is the last time I will ask you to stop the love talk."*

"I don't mean anything by it, just want you to know how much I love you." Rinaldo said.

Gail blocks his phone number and blocks him on social media.

Poor boundary:

> ➢ Rinaldo refuses to accept Gail's 'no' and continues his love bombing.
> ➢ Gail gives up on resisting Rinaldo and gives him what he wants.
> ➢ Gail secretly likes the attention and continues to receive Rinaldo's messages.
> ➢ Gail interprets Rinaldo's love bombing as true love and gives in to him.

Healthy boundary:

> ✓ Rinaldo stops asking Gail to be in a romantic relationship with him.

✓ Gail blocks Rinaldo's phone number and blocks him on social media.

12. Poor self-care

Not valuing your own self-worth and dignity often results in poor self-care. You punish yourself because of someone else's inappropriate or harmful behavior, as if you are responsible for their choices and actions. Poor self-care can also occur in response to someone else's behavior that you misinterpret to be demeaning of you. Poor self-care is expressed in self-neglect, self-harm, and abusing yourself with food and/or substances.

> Cheryl had a rough day at work. After her boss reminded the sales force, which includes Cheryl, of upcoming deadlines to meet their quota, she thought he dressed her down in the department meeting. So after work, she ate a pint of ice cream and a family pack of cookies to feel better. Cheryl later felt guilty for overindulging and developed a stomach ache.

Poor boundary:

➤ Cheryl assumes that her boss targeted her.
➤ Cheryl overindulges in food to cope with her stress.

Healthy boundary:

✓ Cheryl engages in a relaxing activity to calm herself, like yoga, meditation or journaling.
✓ Cheryl limits her snacking to one serving.
✓ Cheryl reflects on her assumption that her boss criticized her in the meeting.

13. Unrealistic guilt

Personalization creates unrealistic guilt, which is another example of taking on someone else's stuff. When you personalize someone else's experience as if it's your own, you try to control their choices and protect them from the consequences of those choices. The unrealistic guilt presents itself when you see yourself as the cause of negative outcomes, blame yourself for another person's bad experiences, or feel guilty about someone else's inappropriate boundaries.

Example 1

Jeremy was late to work often, as late as one hour sometimes. Though Jeremy's tardiness negatively impacted productivity and team morale, his supervisor, Bob, let it slide because Jeremy had a rough life and even told him so on several occasions. Bob has even said, *"I'll cut you some slack this time cause I know how hard things have been for you."* Six months later, Bob's department was under review; the decreased production triggered his manager to call for Jeremy's termination. Bob called in sick to avoid doing so because he "felt bad" for Jeremy.

Poor boundary:

> ➤ Jeremy continues to be tardy and has poor work performance after speaking with Bob.
> ➤ Bob does not hold Jeremy accountable for his behavior--repeated tardiness and not meeting company standards.
> ➤ Bob personalizes Jeremy's situation and behavior.
> ➤ Bob avoids his responsibility as a supervisor by calling in sick.

Healthy boundary:

> ✓ Jeremy improves his attendance and work performance.

- ✓ Bob sets clear job performance requirements and expectations with Jeremy, and applies appropriate consequences when they were not met.
- ✓ Bob shows up and terminates Jeremy as directed by his manager due to Jeremy's ongoing poor work performance and tardiness.

Example 2

Trent's middle son, Jaden, is 32 years old and has lived on his own since graduating from college with a Master of Business Administration degree. He pays his bills and spends a lot of money on games and adult toys, saving little. So when Jaden's company cut his hours, along with other employees, he had difficulty paying his living expenses with no savings to rely on.

Trent felt guilty and blamed himself for Jaden's financial choices, which unfortunately led to Jaden hiding his new truck to avoid repossession. Jaden refused Trent's offer to move in with him because Jaden didn't want to live by his father's rules.

Poor boundary:

- ➢ Trent gives Jaden money to pay his bills.
- ➢ Trent pays Jaden's bills himself.
- ➢ Trent berates himself to figure out where he went wrong as a parent.

Healthy boundary:

- ✓ Trent offers emotional support to Jaden.
- ✓ Trent offers to loan Jaden some money.
- ✓ Jaden evaluates his choices and makes the best one available to him.

14. Allowing Others to Direct Your Life/Experience

This emotional boundary issue represents disinterest in and unwillingness to take responsibility for yourself. This involves assigning your personal control over self to someone else, typically someone you deem smarter, stronger, more attractive, richer, etc. than you are.

> Sherry and Donald dated for two years when they decided to move in together. Donald alone shopped for their new home and chose the neighborhood they'd live in. Sherry asked him no questions about his decisions. Yet, she complained to her best friend that she didn't know what was happening nor what to expect. The friend suggested Sherry ask Donald what she needed to know, such as *Does he want to rent or buy? Will they both be on the lease/mortgage? How will they split the expenses? Whose furniture will they sell?* Sherry responded to her friend's suggestion with, *"I don't want to bother him with details, and I'm sure it'll work out"*, then complained again.

Poor boundary:

> ➢ Sherry is passive and refuses to participate in her own life and future.
> ➢ Sherry continues to complain about not knowing her boyfriend's plans for them.
> ➢ Sherry refuses to self-advocate and ask Donald questions about their life together.

Healthy boundary:

> ✓ Sherry asks Donald about his plans for them.
> ✓ Sherry assertively communicates her own wants and needs to Donald about their life together.

15. Off Limits

Healthy relationships require shared openness. Family and close friends are introduced to partners. Goals and dreams are discussed with partners. The willingness to listen to and understand that the partner's perspective exists. When one partner compartmentalizes an important aspect of his/her/their life and keeps it off limits from the other partner, then poor emotional boundaries are at play.

> Kinsey and her boyfriend dated for 2½ years. In that time, she was not allowed to spend time in his home. He told her at different times that she couldn't visit because his house was dirty, because it was being renovated, and because he was worried about her driving that far to visit him. So when they saw each other, it was always at her house or in public.

Poor boundary:

- ➢ Kinsey accepts being excluded from her boyfriend's home.
- ➢ Kinsey's boyfriend continues to limit her access to his home and private life.

Healthy boundary:

- ✓ Kinsey visits her boyfriend at his home.
- ✓ Kinsey leaves the one-sided relationship if her boyfriend refuses to open his home to her.

16. Excusing Inappropriate Behavior of Others

Excuses provide those with poor boundaries implicit permission to ignore and to continue their harmful actions. Some excuses are: *He means well. She didn't mean it. They were angry. He's under a lot of stress.* Meaning well, not meaning it, being angry, and experiencing stress do not justify inflicting harm on another person.

Greta opened the door to greet her cousin Leonard when he arrived at the family gathering. Instead of reciprocating, Leonard openly yelled at her and called her names in front of others because she didn't wait for him outside like he told her to. When Greta's best friend asked about the incident later, she said, *"He has a lot on his mind. I know he didn't mean what he said."*

Poor boundary:

> ➤ Leonard yells at Greta and calls her names, particularly in front of others.
> ➤ Greta excuses and overlooks Leonard's behavior.

Healthy boundary:

> ✓ Leonard greets Greta then asks her privately why she didn't wait for him outside.
> ✓ Greta doesn't excuse Leonard's behavior and speaks with him about it later in private.

17. People pleasing

Similar to personalization triggering unrealistic guilt, the #13 poor emotional boundary, people pleasing is the strategy to control how other people see and react to you. Basically, the purpose of people pleasing is to receive love and approval, and to prevent others from being angry with you. To that end, you agree to do more than you can possibly handle, you pretend to agree with another's perspective to avoid conflict (i.e., their anger), or you give in and do things that you don't want to. The reality of people pleasing is that you cannot change or control another human being. You only control what you do, say, think, and feel.

Randy is an apprentice with a boss who is emotionally explosive and easily triggered by things that don't go *right* or the way he thinks they should go, like customers only calling when he has free time and Randy just knowing how to do a task without him explicitly explaining it to Randy or demonstrating what to do.

Consequently, Randy is highly anxious and on edge at work. He spends a lot of mental and emotional energy in an attempt to keep his boss from getting angry, trying to control the boss' reactions. So, Randy doesn't ask his boss for specifics about a task and feigns understanding what to do which results in him making mistakes. And his boss gets angry anyway.

Poor boundary:

> Randy doesn't ask his boss what he needs to know about work in an attempt to keep his boss from getting angry.
> Randy attempts to control his boss' emotions.
> Randy takes responsibility for his boss' reactions.

Healthy boundary:

✓ Randy understands that his boss' outbursts are not his responsibility and has no control over him.
✓ Randy is able to separate his boss' behavior from his own self-worth.
✓ Randy appropriately asks his boss for the information and guidance he needs to perform his job effectively.

18. Disproportionate anger

Anger is a natural human emotion that can be triggered by boundary violations, which constitutes appropriate anger. However, when the outburst is way bigger than the trigger, that anger is inappropriate and is often based upon the unrealistic thoughts and expectations of the person having the outburst.

Greg and Bonnie recently moved in together. One evening when they cooked dinner together, Bonnie suggested using one seasoning over another one. Greg threw the potholder on the counter and yelled, *"You never listen to me, always have to have things go your way."*

Poor boundary:

> ➤ Greg throws the potholder.
> ➤ Greg yells at Bonnie.
> ➤ Greg accuses Bonnie of being selfish and controlling.
> ➤ Greg's anger is out of proportion to the situation.

Healthy boundary:

> ✓ Greg agrees to use the seasoning Bonnie suggested.
> ✓ Greg explains to Bonnie why he doesn't want to use the seasoning she suggested.
> ✓ Greg calmly asks why she wants to change the seasoning.

19. Rigid Independence

The unwillingness to ask for and accept help, even when it is appropriate, is rigid independence. Such unrealistic self-reliance is personally limiting and inhibits authentic connection with other human beings. This emotional boundary is a wall with the purpose of keeping *bad* things out, all the while the wall keeps genuine love from getting in.

While shopping for my wedding dress, I saw a suit that I immediately thought would look really good on my first fiancé. And when I told him so on the phone that night, he went off. He snapped, *"I can shop for myself; I don't need you to dress me."*

Poor boundary:

- ➢ The fiancé's anger is an overreaction.
- ➢ The fiancé reflexively rejects my opinion.
- ➢ The fiancé assumes I tried to control him.

Healthy boundary:

- ✓ The fiancé says something along the lines of 'describe it', 'what did you like about it?' 'I'll check it out'.
- ✓ The fiancé says, *"I already picked out my suit."*

20. Stalking

This emotional boundary issue involves imposing your presence on another person via telephone, text, social media, in-person, and in other calculated ways. Examples of stalking include 1) you just *happen* to be at her favorite coffee shop exactly when she is; 2) you *coincidentally* see him arriving at or leaving his job because you have business to do nearby; 3) you call or message them frequently because you want to make sure they're *safe*.

Arina is a client who began dating after her recent divorce. During the second date with the man in whom she was interested, he talked about a work issue with her. He wanted information from his boss who didn't get back with him as quickly as the date wanted, even though the date left him several voicemail messages. So Arina's date told her that he found his boss' address and went to his house one night to get the answers he sought earlier. Arina cringed and felt a pit in her stomach as he described his actions.

Poor boundary:

- ➢ Arina ignores her intuition and rationalizes the date's behavior positively as him being persistent and determined, and continues to see him.

Healthy boundary:

✓ Arina respects her intuition, which leads her to recognize that the date's behavior was stalking and never saw him again.

21. Personalization

Blaming yourself for the negative consequences of other people's choices, attempting to protect others from those consequences, feeling guilty because you couldn't, and sacrificing your health and wellbeing to make others "happy" are forms of personalization. Taking responsibility for other people's choices is based on the belief that you have control over them and you *should have* done or should be able to do something different in order to please or make that person happy. Most certainly, you *should've* done something to keep bad things from happening to that person. This is an unrealistic mindset that often results in anxiety, depression, self-loathing, and inappropriate guilt.

While personalization can trigger unrealistic guilt, emotional boundary red flag #13, and people pleasing, emotional boundary red flag #17, this example of personalization is about attempting to control another person's experience rather than allow them to experience the natural consequences of their choices.

Example 1:

Grace's coworker, Joe, did not take lunch to work on most days. Instead, he would sit across the table in the breakroom from Grace and lay it on thick with comments like, *I don't have money for food today, my girlfriend didn't cook,* and *I can barely afford to keep my lights on.* They worked in a factory and the work was very physical, so Grace "felt bad" for him not having food during his shift. Because she did have lunch, Grace felt responsible for feeding Joe so he wouldn't go hungry all day. She shared her food with him for months whenever they had break at the same time.

As time passed, Grace became angry about *having* to feed Joe and feeling guilty when she thought of saying no to him. In unpacking this with her, Grace admitted that Joe lived with his girlfriend and he often lost money gambling.

Poor boundary:

- ➢ Grace shares her food with Joe regularly when he is capable of providing his own lunch.
- ➢ Grace protects Joe from the natural consequence (hunger) of not taking lunch to work even though he could make other choices that enable him to do so.
- ➢ Joe refuses to prepare or buy his own lunch.
- ➢ Joe refuses to ask his live-in girlfriend to prepare food for him.

Healthy boundary:

- ✓ Grace says 'no' to sharing her lunch with Joe.
- ✓ Grace stops enabling Joe to be irresponsible in fulfilling his own need to eat.
- ✓ Joe takes his own lunch to work.

Example 2:

Phoebe has a son who is in his 30s. He received a less than favorable employee evaluation because of significant errors he made. When Phoebe's son told her about his review, she blamed herself for being a bad parent because if she were a good one, then her son would not have received that review. Phoebe ate 2 bags of potato chips to comfort herself.

Poor boundary:

- ➢ Phoebe blames herself for her son's job performance.
- ➢ Phoebe engages in emotional eating to avoid her inappropriate guilt.

Healthy boundary:

- ✓ Phoebe stops taking responsibility for her son's choices and behavior.
- ✓ Phoebe stops making excuses for her son's poor work performance.
- ✓ Phoebe empathizes with her son and listens to his needs.
- ✓ Phoebe's son improves his job performance.

Example 3:

Kera's mother drank excessively after divorcing her husband, Kera's father. The mother's drinking basically incapacitated her to the point where Kera, who was only 10, took on the care of her younger sibling, age 5. Kera blamed herself and felt guilty for her parents' divorce and mother's excessive drinking. She believed then that had she been a better daughter earlier, her parents would not have divorced and her mother would not have become an alcoholic, which left Kera to parent herself and her younger sibling. Now in her 40s, Kera still believes this.

Poor boundary:

- ➢ Kera blames herself for her parents' divorce.
- ➢ Kera blames herself for her mother's drinking.

Healthy boundary:

- ✓ Kera identifies and does what she could to nurture herself and her sibling.
- ✓ Kera accepts that she is not responsible for her parents' choices and behavior.
- ✓ Kera's self-worth and self-confidence remain intact despite her family situation.

22. Proving yourself

The need to prove yourself to someone comes from the position of believing the other person is the standard or are right, even though you disagree with them. This position often results in the faulty beliefs of *I'm not good enough, I'm unlovable, I'm not worthy.* These faulty, unrealistic, beliefs trigger rebellion and the need to defend your opinions and your choices, which is simply the need to prove yourself right. Rebellion and non-conformity are often about the external and how one presents, either in vocabulary, mannerisms, geography, or appearance – hair color, clothing, and the like.

The need to prove yourself right or to prove that you are good enough comes from the belief that you are not either, which creates an internal struggle of desiring to be unique and needing to conform in order to be accepted and loved. The be yourself or be loved mindset is a false narrative that invalidates your worth. Your worth as a human being exists outside and independently of this false narrative that was imposed upon you. It's only a matter of seeing the narrative and defining your own path, even if your path resembles that of which you rebel against.

However, if the external change is not matched with a shift in your mindset, then proving yourself to be unlike them is fruitless because the internal comparisons remain--what you rebel against is still your measuring stick for value and worth.

Example 1:

Zach comes from a financially well-off family. His parents often used money to pressure him and his siblings to obey them, including life and partner choices that only the parents approved of. Growing up, Zach often thought to himself that he would not use money to control people.

As an educated, intelligent, and responsible 40-something adult, Zach has deliberately chosen low-paying jobs. His justification for limiting himself career-wise and financially is because he didn't want to be like his parents. He equated wealth with control. So, to not be controlling like his parents, he chose to be working poor and live paycheck-to-paycheck.

Poor boundary:

> Zach rebels against his parents by taking low-paying jobs.
> Zach equates controlling behavior with having money.
> Zack limits his potential to prove he isn't like his controlling parents.

Healthy boundary:

✓ Zach accepts good-paying jobs as long as they align with his goals, desires, and skills.
✓ Zach learns about healthy relationships and how to identify controlling behaviors to avoid and to correct.

Example 2:

Linda was raised in a strict, religious home. She and her siblings were required to dress modestly, to stand a measured distance away from the opposite sex, were taught to be seen rather than heard, and were punished for expressing their interests outside of traditional gender roles, like girls playing sports and boys wanting to cook.

Linda left home at age 19 because she couldn't take the restrictions any longer. Living on her own, Linda embraced freedom from her parents' tyranny and wore shirts that showed her cleavage, mini-skirts, short shorts, and stilettos.

This new wardrobe drew the type of attention that Linda was uncomfortable with because it was from people she found creepy and sexually suggestive. Even though Linda did not enjoy this attention, she continued to dress that way because she didn't live with her parents anymore and could wear anything she wanted.

Poor boundary:

> ➤ Linda dresses the exact opposite way of her parents' rules because she could.
> ➤ Linda continues to dress in ways she is personally uncomfortable with.

Healthy boundary:

> ✓ Linda develops her own style and self-expression, not just do the opposite of what her mother and father told her to do.
> ✓ Linda understands and accepts her parents' positive and realistic teachings.

22. Gaslighting

Gaslighting is a form of emotional abuse. It involves a pattern of intentionally negative behavior for the purpose of gaining control over someone or a situation by making the person question their own thoughts, their memory, their sanity, and their sense of reality. Some tactics used by gaslighters include deception, manipulation, creating confusion, negative labels, and denial even when confronted with "evidence". So while you're off balance and busy defending yourself or apologizing, the one who does the gaslighting escapes responsibility for their actions.

Erica and her fiancé have been together 3 years. They don't live together and at this point, Erica doesn't want to because he demeans her career field, blames her for his failures, and berates her when she makes suggestions about everyday tasks like cooking and home organization. And she has had several conversations with him about his behavior to no avail. After speaking with her trusted confidant about it, Erica was certain that breaking up was the right choice for her.

A few days later, Erica again spoke with her fiancé about his behavior. He told her that she's not trying hard enough to make things work and she doesn't give him a chance to do anything right. Erica was then confused about leaving him and worried that she was not doing enough or patient enough to make their relationship work. Vacillating between staying and leaving increases Erica's anxiety, as does going from being clear about her needs in the relationship to second guessing herself.

Inherent in healthy relationships is clarity. Erica's confusion is the red flag.

Poor boundary:

> ➤ Erica ignores her own experience and needs to please her fiancé.
> ➤ Erica accepts her fiancé's perspective as her reality.

Healthy boundary:

> ✓ Erica respects her experience with her fiancé as invalidating and made her decision accordingly.
> ✓ Erica stops accepting her fiancé's criticisms of her as reality.

SUMMARY

Even though emotional boundaries lack the clarity that's inherent in physical, mental, and spiritual boundaries, you can still learn how to identify them. Allow the examples of emotional boundary violations in this chapter to teach you how to see the red flags in real time and give yourself the best opportunities to protect and nurture yourself.

Emotional Boundary Activity

Answer the questions below to assess your emotional boundary.

Who do you try to rescue from bad things, negative consequences?

_____

Are you successful at saving him/her/them? □ Yes   □ No

Do you feel capable of handling your own life? □ Yes   □ No

If no, then who takes charge of your life?

_____

Are you happy and fulfilled with this person in control of your experience?   □ Yes   □ No

CHAPTER 7

SEEING PHYSICAL, MENTAL, AND SPIRITUAL BOUNDARY RED FLAGS

"I wish the pain of betrayal was as easy to ignore as the red flags that forewarned it."
—Steve Maraboli

Below are a few examples of how red flags, the warning signs of boundary violations, look in real time so you can have more clarity about how they present in real life. Each scenario is identified by the type of boundary it is —physical, mental, and spiritual, along with examples of how the healthy and unhealthy boundary can present behaviorally.

PHYSICAL BOUNDARY RED FLAGS

Your physical boundaries are about your body and what happens to it. Your frame, skin, and the immediate space around your body are natural barriers between you and other people.

Cringing

Whenever you're around a certain person, you experience dread, uneasiness, and negative physical sensations like cringing or the hairs on the back of your neck stand on end. These reactions alert you that potential harm is near.

The husband of Marcia's best friend "accidently" touched her breast as he walked by her. He apologized with a wink. Since, being around him gives Marcia the heebie jeebies so she keeps her distance whenever she is around them and avoids being alone with him.

Poor boundary:

> ➢ Marcia excuses the husband's behavior – it was an accident and he didn't mean anything by it or I was standing in his way.
> ➢ Marcia ignores her discomfort and pretends nothing happened, potentially putting herself in harm's way again.

Healthy boundary:

> ✓ Marcia speaks to the husband and requests that he not touch her.
> ✓ Marcia protects her physical space by keeping her distance from the husband.
> ✓ Marcia avoids being alone with the husband.
> ✓ Marcia limits contact with her friend and her husband.

Body Language

While spoken words are an important part of communication, the non-verbal cues are just as important in authentic communication. Body language often reveals more than words do because of the emotional energy inherent in it. Eye contact is one of the most telling elements of non-verbal cues.

A group of friends invited Benson to their Sunday social. Amber noticed that Benson rarely made eye contact with anyone, even when spoken to directly the first time he attended their social. She was uncomfortable with it and talked about it with her boyfriend afterward. They decided that Benson must be shy. Several socials later, Benson continued lowering his eyes when interacting with the group.

Amber brought it up in the group when Benson was not present. Others admitted that they too were uncomfortable with it and realized that Benson somehow escaped paying his share of the tab.

Poor boundary:

> ➢ Benson doesn't make eye contact.
> ➢ Benson doesn't pay his share of the tab.
> ➢ The group continues to make excuses for Benson's behavior.

Healthy boundary:

> ✓ Group members ask Benson about his lack of eye contact.
> ✓ Group members remind Benson to pay his share of the bill or drop him from their social group.
> ✓ Group members express to Benson their concerns re: lack of eye contact when they're communicating with him.

Chapter 14, Communicating Your Boundaries Non-verbally, provides more information about and examples of body language.

Unwanted Touching

Your body, shape, size, and frame comprise your natural physical boundary and barrier of protection, if you will. When someone touches you without your consent or continues to do so even after you express not wanting it, and allowing someone to touch you or stand closer than is comfortable for you are violations of your physical boundary.

Sabrina complained to her husband about a coworker, Raj. She didn't like Raj standing close and putting his hand on her shoulder whenever they reviewed client accounts. Sabrina rolled her shoulder as if to shrug him off then stiffened her upper body, hoping that Raj would get the hint and stop touching her. He didn't. So, she began avoiding meetings with him which negatively affected her job performance.

Poor boundary:

> ➢ Sabrina does not speak up for herself to Raj.
> ➢ Sabrina does not seek guidance and support from her supervisor nor human resources.
> ➢ Sabrina hopes Raj would get it on his own and stop touching her.
> ➢ Raj thinks it was okay to stand close to Sabrina.
> ➢ Raj touches Sabrina without her consent.

Healthy boundary:

> ✓ Sabrina asks Raj to keep a comfortable distance from her.
> ✓ Sabrina asks Raj to stop touching her.
> ✓ Sabrina sets up meetings with Raj to review client files across a table rather than side-by-side.
> ✓ Sabrina consults with her supervisor and/or human resources about the situation.

Blocking

Blocking is another form of violating the physical boundary. Even though the violator doesn't touch inappropriately or with violence, restricting another person's freedom to move physically is the violation -- you block her path or the door to keep her from leaving, you grab their phone to keep them from calling for help, or you hide his keys so he can't drive away.

One client moved to another state to be with a man she met online two weeks prior. He was very charming and offered her a good life where she would have everything she needed to be happy. This man was the only person she knew in the state. While he was at work, she walked around to familiarize herself with the area and to get fresh air. When he became aware of her walks, he locked her inside and took her phone whenever he left home without her.

Poor boundary:

> ➤ The man isolates her by locking her in and taking her phone.
> ➤ The woman makes the quick commitment to this man before getting to know him.

Healthy boundary:

> ✓ She takes more time to get to know him before leaving her home state and moving in with him.
> ✓ She strengthens her relationship with herself so she would be less vulnerable to such promises.
> ✓ She leaves that relationship to regain her self-confidence and freedom to move about.

Physical Violence

This red flag is about overt control. Laying hands on another person includes the intent to control and cajole obedience, which is antithetical to healthy relationships. Some examples involve slapping, punching, kicking, pushing, pinching, blocking the path or door, and holding on to someone physically. Typically, the overt control is subtle in the beginning of relationships then escalates over time.

Klara's new husband was the man of her dreams because he was charming and attentive. Yet, she overlooked his unexplained absences when they dated. Married, he also arrived home late most nights and without explanation. When Klara asked where he had been, he initially responded with, *"I was takin care of business"* or *"Just hangin with friends"*. His vague answers soon gave way to *"Don't question me woman, you focus on taking care of the kids"*.

Because of his reactions, Klara stopped questioning him about his whereabouts. Then when she saw a text on his phone from another woman thanking him for the intimate things they'd done the night before, Klara couldn't help but confront him with it. She angrily asked who the woman was and about their affair. He grabbed Klara's arm and yelled, *"I told you don't question me. I'm the man of the house and you do what I say."*

"I'm your wife. I have a right to know." She implored. He slapped Klara then pushed her down.

Poor Boundary:

> ➤ The husband is dishonest and unfaithful.
> ➤ The husband is abusive to Klara.
> ➤ Klara ignored the red flags of his absences during their dating period.

Healthy Boundary:

> ✓ The husband manages his anger and does not hit Klara.
> ✓ The husband is faithful.
> ✓ Klara honestly reflects on her situation and chooses safety for her and her children.

MENTAL BOUNDARY RED FLAGS

Betrayal and Flaking

You, your partner, friend, or family member renege on commitments. Betrayal and flaking are forms of mental boundary violations that occur when someone does not keep their agreements and does not communicate with the other party when their situation changes which prohibits them from following through on the commitment they made.

Betrayal and flaking also occur when someone consistently says *yes* then cancels at the last minute, doesn't show up, doesn't take your calls, or doesn't respond to your messages or attempts to contact them. These violations can trigger anger in the person who is betrayed and left waiting.

Jimmy was in therapy to address his depression which developed from his father's broken promises. The dad worked a lot and when not working, he hung out with his friends. Seeing the disappointment on Jimmy's face before leaving the house, his father promised to take him to the amusement park, to a ball game, to the movies, or do something with him the next weekend. And Jimmy got excited again. When that time arrived, however, Jimmy's father had something else important to do and again canceled on Jimmy. This negative pattern of broken promises, agreements, resulted in Jimmy believing that he is unlovable and unworthy because his father did not spend much time with him, which led to his depression.

Poor Boundary:

> ➤ Jimmy's father doesn't keep his promises.
> ➤ Jimmy's father continues to make empty promises.
> ➤ Jimmy continues to believe his father's broken promises.
> ➤ Jimmy faults himself for his father's betrayals.

Healthy Boundary:

> ✓ Jimmy's father stops making false promises.
> ✓ Jimmy sets real expectations for his father.

✓ Jimmy recognizes that his father's behavior is not a reflection of his self-worth.

Expectations

The flip side of agreements is expectations--what you presume or anticipate someone else will do and when they'll do it to achieve the agreed upon goal. Agreements determine what each party in the agreement expects of the other person. In the example above, Jimmy's father made agreements that he did not keep, like taking Jimmy to ball games. Yet, Jimmy continued to expect his father to come through. His expectation of his father was unrealistic; it was false hope that his father would keep a promise, which set Jimmy up for mental health issues because he questioned his worth as a son.

In another example, my first husband had unrealistic expectations of me. Four months into our agreed upon separation, he was served with divorce papers. As the divorce neared finalization, he and I had a telephone conversation about dividing up possessions. I gave him first choice of furniture and furnishings. On the phone, he was hostile and combative toward me, changing the subject and his selections frequently. Finally, I stopped going back and forth with him then asked him to make a decision to stop this.

He replied, *"You led me on. You made me believe we would get back together."* What? I took a deep breath then responded, *"I never said I love you. I never said I miss you. I never said let's talk about it or work it out. And I never asked to see you. So where did you get that from?"* He didn't answer. After being silent for a few moments, he must have realized that his expectation of us getting back together was unrealistic. He then was decisive about what items he would take and agreed on a date to pick them up.

SPIRITUAL BOUNDARY RED FLAGS

Values and Principals

The Spiritual Boundary is about the alignment of your values and principles with your choices. When you go against your principles and values to please someone else, to gain something, or to do what's easiest or fastest, then you trigger an internal struggle between your ego and your Personal Truth. This struggle often presents as anxiety, depression, self-loathing, hopelessness, and even self-harm.

Example 1:

Many American constituents proclaim to believe in family values and law and order. Yet, they endorse and elect known adulterers and convicted criminals to positions of leadership in the government on both the federal and state levels. Politicians who have been caught having affairs, possessing and using drugs, securing illegal financial and material gains from their positions, and other criminal acts are repeatedly elected and reelected by voters.

The stated beliefs of family values and law and order do not align with the voters' choices of criminal and unethical elected officials.

Poor boundary:

➢ Voters elect criminal and unethical leaders, going against their proclaimed values and principles.

Healthy boundary:

✓ Voters research candidates and vote for the ones most aligned with their stated principles and values.

Example 2:

Zoey was 17 when she started dating Shawn, who was 32. He encouraged her to keep their relationship a secret, explaining that no one would understand their love because of the age difference. Zoey resisted keeping the secret because she was proud to be with him, wanted to share their love with her family and friends, and she did not lie to her parents, with whom she lived. Shawn promised to reveal their relationship when the time was right. Unfortunately, Zoey finally gave in to his persistence even though she felt guilty and ashamed for lying to her parents and friends when she disappeared to be with Shawn.

Poor boundary:

> ➢ Zoey changes and lies to loved ones to please Shawn by keeping their relationship a secret.

Healthy boundary:

> ✓ Zoey is honest with her parents and best friend about Shawn.
> ✓ Zoey doesn't lie about her whereabouts when with Shawn.

Example 3:

Klara, from the Physical Violence example above, was religious, believed in the nuclear family, and believed that the man as head of household would take care of and do the right things for his family. Yet, she clung to her husband who was controlling, abusive, and a philanderer.

Poor boundary:

> ➢ Klara marries a man who does not align with her beliefs and values.
> ➢ Klara stays married to her husband after learning that he had affairs and after he is physically violent

with her—behaviors that do not align with her values and principles.

Healthy boundary:

- ✓ Klara accepts that her husband is not aligned with her spiritual beliefs and makes the appropriate decisions to prioritize her and her children's health and wellbeing.

Example 4:

For more than a year, Nancy was one of my coworkers when I lived in another state. We got along well, discussed many topics, and consistently had positive interactions even though she made many references to good/evil, right/wrong. I checked in with her a few times when she had difficulties in her family. On more than one occasion, Nancy told me that I was a kind and giving person, and she could see my light. Then one day when standing in my office, she asked what church I attended because for her I couldn't be kind and considerate without church. I answered that I did not go to church. Nancy's body stiffened, her nose lifted into the air, and she walked out in a huff.

Days later, Nancy expressed her dismay to me and basically told me that I was going to hell. I asked, *"So I'm no longer a good person?"* She made a sound that conveyed indignation then said, *"If you were a good person then you'd go to church"*. I responded with, *"Are you judging me?"* Nancy walked away again.

About a month later, Nancy apologized to me and admitted that she did judge me, which didn't align with her religion. Our relationship was never the same again, however.

Poor boundary:

- ➢ I ignore Nancy's black and white references thinking they didn't apply to me.
- ➢ Nancy judges me.
- ➢ Nancy attempts to emotionally blackmail me in order to coerce me to go to church.

Healthy boundary:

- ✓ I recognize Nancy's good vs evil thinking and keep a professional distance from her.
- ✓ Nancy seeks to understand my beliefs rather than judge me.
- ✓ Nancy accepts my life choices.

The example below wreaks of mental and emotional red flags, as it involves several warning signs.

After my divorce, I tried online dating. An attractive man expressed interest in me so I checked out his profile. He presented as an interesting and stable guy with similar interests. I clicked on "mutual attraction". That's the way it was done at the time, no swiping right or left ☺. He then messaged me. Now, I didn't stay on the site for long nor did I check my messages every day. And when I logged in again a day or so later, I saw that he sent a polite message not long after I selected the match and logged off. Then I was unpleasantly surprised by his second message: *"I thought you would've responded by now."* The timestamp of the second message was just two hours after his first one. The angry tone and demand in this message set off my alarm bells.

Poor boundary:

- ➢ He expects an immediate reply from me.
- ➢ He overreacts with anger when I didn't meet his expectations and reply sooner.

> ➤ I experience guilt for disappointing him.
> ➤ I attempt to please him by apologizing and trying to make it up to him.

Healthy boundary:

> ✓ I respond calmly and neutrally.
> ✓ I heed the red flag of his overreaction and don't reply at all.
> ✓ I reply that I changed my mind about matching with him.

SUMMARY

Hopefully you noticed that the above examples of unhealthy boundaries reveal boundary issues internally and externally, inside and outside of you. Being able to identify how boundaries present from your perspective and from others will heighten your awareness of boundary violations in real time, giving you a great opportunity to act to protect yourself.

Note that some situations involve more than one boundary issue, such as the emotional boundary of people-pleasing and the spiritual boundary of values and principals in the examples above. Once you're able to see red flags, next comes your response. What you do with the red flags determines the health of your boundaries with that individual, group, or situation. Some people will make excuses for the inappropriate or harmful behavior, justify or rationalize why they should ignore them. However, trusting your gut will help guide you through this process. Read more about intuition in the next chapter, Intuiting Your Boundaries and Relationships.

Seeing Red Flags Activity

Describe 5 physical, mental, or spiritual red flags that you have experienced and who was involved.

1. _____

2. _____

3. _____

4. _____

5. _____

In which relationships in your life do these 5 signs of unhealthy boundaries occur most often? Check all that apply:

☐ Spouse / Partner
☐ Sibling / Relative
☐ Parent / Child
☐ Boss / Coworker
☐ Other

CHAPTER 8

INTUITING YOUR BOUNDARIES AND RELATIONSHIPS

"In simple everyday decision making, intuition gives everyone an edge. When we feel stuck and uncertain, it's often because we are only seeing a part of the whole. A flash of intuition illuminates everything. We see the big picture and an array of options we never saw before."
—Marcia Emery, Ph.D.

I'll go a bit further than Marcia and say that your intuition is designed to deliver to you an advantage in protecting and nurturing self. Intuition is a gift and is innate for human beings, which means that you have this inner wisdom too. And your intuition provides insight into your safety and guidance for self-care and self-actualization. Are you listening to it? Unfortunately, too many people ignore their intuition because they can't see it or touch it and assign their power to others, like assigning Medicare benefits to a Health Maintenance Organization (HMO).

Your intuition is the link to a knowing that transcends physical evidence and the intellect, which is misguidedly used as the 'reason' to disregard it. Nonetheless, your intuition serves to promote your best self in many ways. As such, your intuition nourishes your creativity, inspiration, and awareness, and it affirms your healthy choices.

"Communication between the personality and its soul is an in-house intuitive process."

The previous chapters on seeing red flags planted the seed of how unhealthy boundaries are displayed in real time. To give you an intellectual heads-up if you will. This chapter describes the ways in which your intuition warns you during a red flag. Let me remind you that the primary purposes of intuition are self-protection and nurturing by means of monitoring your innate alarm system, which is comprised of your boundaries. Some refer to intuition as an *instinct* or a *hunch.* And for some, intuition presents as a soft or commanding voice, as a powerful thought, as a strong nudge, or as an immediate knowing.

> *"It [intuition] is knowing without knowing why."*
> —Gavin De Becker

Let me share a few examples of intuition.

Go Back

I met a friend at the new T-Mobile Arena in Las Vegas for an event, arriving by rideshare. After the event, she and I separated at the new rideshare pickup area which was different from the drop off spot and which was operated by a rideshare company different from the one I used. My friend went to the Excalibur to get a cab. I stayed at the pickup area and waited for the rideshare I requested. Unfortunately, my rideshare company could not find the pickup spot. So after I was assigned and reassigned several drivers because they couldn't find the new and remote location I was in, I walked down the street to get a better signal so the Global Positioning System (GPS) could help drivers successfully navigate to my pin on the map.

I stood there on a dark corner next to the I-15 freeway holding my phone up to get a strong signal so the rideshare drivers could find me. A few minutes passed when I received a firm message via the thought, *"Go back."* I turned and headed back to the rideshare pickup area without hesitation. As I walked away, I looked over my right shoulder and saw a man arrive at the corner where I stood just seconds before. I imagined what could've happened had I ignored my intuition and stayed there with him walking up behind me, then I thanked God for the intuitive message.

Run

Actress Gabrielle Union has been open about being raped at age 19 by a former employee of the company she worked for at the time. She recounts in Glamour Magazine that "something" telling her to run was suppressed by racial camaraderie, "good home training", and being a "polite" woman.

> *When the man first walked in, I was straightening a display of fake Timberlands. He came up behind me and asked about the boots. I took one look at him and wanted to run, but I didn't. I was aware of how my coworkers and the people in our mostly white community viewed black people, so my racial solidarity and "good home training" as a "polite" woman kicked in.*

> *At 8:45 I started vacuuming. The vacuum was loud, but I still heard Goth Girl scream for me to come to the register. Something in her voice told me to run; again, I didn't. I walked to the front, where the man was holding a gun on her.*

Gabrielle goes on to describe the rape she endured and how she survived the attack. She also shared that she learned in therapy to stop overriding herself by keeping harmful people in her life.

> *"After that I started trusting my instincts. If someone lacked decency or respect, I didn't allow that person to stay in my world."*
> —Gabrielle Union, Oprah.com

First Mind

Have you ever said to yourself, *I should've followed my first mind?* If yes, it was then you realized that your *first mind*, your intuition, was right. Perhaps you can relate to an example about driving. How many times did you ignore your thoughts about going down or avoiding one particular street, only to run into a traffic jam or worse?

> A coworker was livid by the time she arrived at work. She explained that 'something' told her to take the street instead of the freeway when she left home that morning. Yet, she ignored it and then ran into a severe traffic jam. At a complete stop, my coworker turned on the radio for news. She learned that there had been an accident involving a semi-truck and its chemical load spilled onto the freeway, so the freeway was completely shut down. The coworker was stuck in a 3-mile backup that made her arrive to work two hours late.

SUMMARY

The First Mind, your intuition, is present when driving, when meeting new people, when cooking, when shopping, etc. Your intuition is active and accessible to you all day, every day. It's only a matter of paying attention to it so you can become aware of the best opportunity to protect and nurture yourself, and to make the best choices available to you at any given moment.

> *"When you notice someone does something toxic the first time, don't wait for the second time before you address it or cut them off. Many survivors are used to the 'wait and see' tactic which only leaves them vulnerable to a second attack. As your boundaries*

get stronger, the wait time gets shorter. You never
have [to] justify your intuition."
—Shahida Arabi

8.1: Intuiting Your Boundaries Activity

A. Describe 3 situations when you ignored your intuition:

_____

1. How did it work out for you?

_____

2. How did it work out for you?

_____

3. How did it work out for you?

_____

B. Describe 3 situations when you heeded your intuition:

_____

1. How did it work out for you?

_____

2. How did it work out for you?

_____

3. How did it work out for you?

_____

What's your takeaway from following vs ignoring your intuition?

CHAPTER 9

UNDERSTANDING THE TRUTHS ABOUT BOUNDARIES

"Hurt people are not going to stop hurting other people until they receive the memo that it is wrong, or if there are actual consequences for their behavior. Feeling sorry for them and understanding where they 'came from' is not helping to stop the cycle of abuse."
—Darlene Ouimet

The truths about boundaries are their unchanging characteristics. While healthy boundaries are flexible and contextual, they are also paradoxically the same. Understanding the truths about boundaries provides you with an extra layer of empowerment because it takes the guess work out of the who, what, when, where, and for how long. More on these facets of boundaries in the next chapter, Living in Context with your Boundaries. So let's go.

BOUNDARY TRUTH #1

Have you ever asked yourself *"Why does he keep doing that to me?"*

The answer is because they can. We humans tend to continue doing what we can get away with. You see, most people do not self-correct, even when they see that their actions are problematic and hurtful to others. Think of the batterer who promises to never hit his partner again every time he hits her. He can see that his assault is damaging and causes her pain. Yet, he does not change his behavior nor does he even address his underlying issues to make the appropriate corrections.

Consequences are required to affect behavior. Most people do not self-correct without them. And the consequences can be positive, negative, or neutral. Positive consequences reinforce appropriate or desired behavior, such as rewarding your teenager for getting good grades or leaving a big tip for an excellent waiter. On the other hand, negative consequences deter unwanted and inappropriate conduct. Think of the penal system--taking away a person's freedom to give them time to reflect on their actions that led to incarceration with the goal of them learning to choose appropriate and legal behaviors when released. Another example of a negative consequence is suspending an employee without pay who is chronically late to work.

Note here that neutral consequences don't generate the emotional energy of positive and negative consequences. Instead, you can consider the neutral outcome of any choice as 'no harm done'.

In reflecting on the question, *"Why does he keep doing that?"*, consider what consequences you have implemented and how effective they were in either reinforcing acceptable behavior or discouraging inappropriate and harmful behavior.

Boundary Truth #1: People will continue to do what they're allowed to get away with.

BOUNDARY TRUTH #2

Have you ever said to yourself *"It's gotten worse."* Or *"It was never this bad."*?

If you have, then you noticed the escalation of unwanted behavior. The more people get away with their harmful, hurtful, illegal, or problematic behavior, the bolder they get. Then their actions naturally get worse. Without appropriate consequences, humans push the limits of what they're allowed to do and get away with, which leads to the escalation.

Think of the police officers in 2020 and those in 2023 who beat unarmed black men to death, in public and on film. According to news reports, at least two of the officers had histories of excessive force complaints against them without consequences. Those prior complaints serve as examples of escalating behavior. These officers progressed from punching to killing.

Another example of escalating behavior is Klarissa and her husband Roy. After they dated for a few months, Roy began explaining to Klarissa how much he missed her when she went to the gym to work out and how much he loved being with her without her kids from her first marriage. When she countered with wanting to stay healthy and fit, and needing to be there for her kids, especially the preteen, Roy *reminded* her how he felt about it often. Klarissa thought talking about it was enough for him to understand her point of view and to stop guilt-tripping her. Then five years into their marriage, Roy went from explaining to demanding that she spend more time with him. He hid her keys, called her multiple times when she went to the gym, and embarrassed her when her children were present.

Boundary Truth #2: Human behavior unchecked, escalates.

BOUNDARY TRUTH #3

Do you find yourself hoping for or giving in to someone stronger, smarter, better looking, or richer to take care of you?

Some people believe they are incapable of taking care of themselves. So they assign their power to another person who appears to be more confident, more intelligent, more beautiful, and more wealthy in hopes that this savior will give them meaning or purpose. What tends to happen instead is the savior will likely be domineering, controlling, and/or abusive.

> A woman who called herself a "bad ass" at work fell prey to her ex-husband. She did what he said and what he wanted even when doing so went against her intuition and her better judgement simply because he appeared stronger. She did not speak up, self-advocate, nor say "no" when it was appropriate. In attempting to understand how she could effectively manage employees and have successful outcomes at work, she criticized herself for being "weak" when it comes to romantic partners.

Boundary Truth #3: The way you manage your boundaries and treat yourself teaches other people how to treat you.

BOUNDARY TRUTH #4

Do you believe that all you have to do is say "no" to assert your boundaries? As discussed earlier, you wear your boundaries like a second skin and healthy boundaries involve far more than just saying no. In wearing your boundaries, they are integral in how you carry yourself and in your actions.

Speaking and uttering words are only a small part of effective communication. Non-verbal cues also have a significant impact on what you convey. The greatest bearing on effective communication is when what you do matches your words. So don't continue to frustrate yourself by asking *"How many times do I have to say no?"* At this point, stop telling them and show them.

My favorite example of this truth is actress Ashley Judd. She came out during the #metoo movement and told her story.

> Ashley met with a powerful film producer in a hotel room to discuss her potential role in an upcoming movie. He made

several sexual advances toward her, to which she said no repeatedly. Still, he persisted. So, after having her "no" ignored over and over again, Ashley left the hotel room.

Ashley put her no into action. She physically left the situation. Far too often, people, especially women, continue to talk, to speak their boundaries. However, when others push back because they don't like the limits placed upon them no matter how appropriate those limits are, the boundary setter must behave their boundaries as Ashley did. Her final no was walking out and away from danger.

Boundary Truth #4: *No* is not enough. You must behave your boundaries.

BOUNDARY TRUTH #5

Think you need permission to develop, strengthen, or enforce your boundaries? Think again. You do not need permission from another human being to nurture or to protect yourself. You are inherently empowered to do so. It's only a matter of awakening to this power within.

Boundaries are innate. They provide the means by which you protect the integrity of your person and cultivate your best self. Because your boundaries are your innate alarm system, no human need grant you permission to employ them nor can anyone take them away. However, abusive, controlling, and narcissistic people are very skilled at chipping away at your self-worth, your self-confidence, and your resolve to get you to do what they want. Your highest good is not their concern.

An example of nurturing and empowering oneself is that of Janet Jackson. She recognized that she was in charge of her life and set out to define her own reality at the very young age of 18.

The youngest of the very talented musical family, Janet was not in control of her career initially. Joe Jackson, her father and manager, was in charge and made decisions that she did not want for herself. So, Janet fired her father after her first album. She then forged her own identity with the second album, *Control*, which has sold over 10 million copies worldwide. Janet did not beg him to listen to her nor did she wait to see what he would do for her. She took charge of her own life and career, and began making decisions for herself.

Boundary Truth #5: You are already empowered to protect and to nurture yourself.

SUMMARY

Understanding and accepting the truths about boundaries will empower and assist you in making the difficult decisions about who you allow to have a front row seat in your life, when, and for how long. Sometimes, distancing yourself from someone you like or *feel sorry for* is the best choice or leaving a situation in which you are harmed is necessary for your health and safety. Knowing that these truths can simplify your choices and make following through on them easier.

SECTION III:
LIVING IN CONTEXT

This section delves into the contextual nature of boundaries. The popular perception of boundaries is that they are all or nothing, always on or always off. Such black and white thinking is unrealistic and fodder for harm because both extremes are ripe with unnecessary vulnerability. Understanding that boundary issues can vary depending upon the context within which they occur further empowers you to nurture and to protect yourself in real time.

CHAPTER 10

LIVING IN CONTEXT WITH YOUR BOUNDARIES

"Daring to set boundaries is about having the courage to love ourselves even when we risk disappointing others."
—Brene Brown

Somehow, boundaries have gotten the bad rap of being walls. My guess is that this negative reputation came from someone who dislikes having limits placed on them. When I think of mental and emotional walls, I imagine impenetrable structures. Healthy boundaries are not walls nor are they solid. The truth is that healthy boundaries are contextual; they open, close, narrow, and widen as warranted.

I find it helpful to conceptualize the contextual nature of boundaries as a theatre. You are the performer on stage and you assign seats to audience members based upon the boundaries you have with each individual. It's up to you where each person sits and how long they can occupy that seat.

Although you may have firm boundaries that apply across the board, like you don't loan money to family or friends, the boundaries you set are wholly responsive to who, what, when, where, and how long. Let's take a look at each element of context.

Who is the person you are dealing with. Your history, agreements, and patterns with this person all factor into what you allow this person to get and get away with.

What is the situation you're involved in with the *who*. What, the specifics of a situation, can determine your level of tolerance of certain behaviors from other people.

When is all about timing, which *"is everything"* according to William Shakespeare. Choices and behaviors vary depending upon the time when they occur.

Where is about location, location, location. The place at which you interact with a particular person or persons at a specific time also impacts the boundaries you set and affirm.

How Long is different from timing. It is the duration of the interaction you allow or disallow.

You may ask how come "why" is not in this list of boundary contexts. Well, it's because "why" is inherent in all boundary contexts...to protect and nurture self on the physical, mental, emotional, and spiritual levels.

EXAMPLES OF CONTEXTUAL BOUNDARIES

1. It was 6 months after working with Cameron and Denise when I learned they were married. Their boundaries were that good. Cameron and Denise did not display affection nor did they use terms of endearment with each other while on the job. They did however, behave like a couple during work-related social events.

    Who: *Spouse*
    What: *Affection, terms of endearment*
    When: *9-5, work hours*
    Where: *@Work, on the job*
    How long: *the entire work day, while on the job*

2. My nickname was cute growing up. In adulthood, however, being called by my nickname in the presence of anyone who

wasn't around me when I was a child, especially business associates, became inappropriate. So I set the boundary for family and friends to call me Glen in public, at my events, and on social media.

Who: *Family and friends*
What: *Calling me by my nickname*
When: *Anytime when around business associates, colleagues, friends*
Where: *In public, at events, and on social media*
How long: *forever*

3. Jennifer and Jimmy get along and communicate well with each other. However, even the most loving couples argue and need their space to calm and reset. So during an argument, Jennifer does not want to be affectionate with Jimmy because touch at that time feels calculated and disingenuous to her. So Jennifer needs time to process her emotions and get clear enough to maturely address their problem.

Who: *Spouse, significant other*
What: *Affection*
When: *During an argument*
Where: *Anywhere*
How long: *While she is angry/emotional*

4. Gia, a trained and licensed massage therapist, set clear professional boundaries with clients. Because of the confusion between professional massage and prostitution disguised as legitimate massage, one of Gia's boundaries is a ban on any comments or jokes by clients about sex while they are on the massage table, in her office, and on the phone when scheduling.

Who: *Clients*
What: *Comments, jokes, or references about sex*

When: *Before or during a massage, and in reference to massage*
Where: *In her office, on the massage table, on the phone*
How long: *entire session, time in office, during interactions re: massage*

5. Micaela and Gloria have been good friends for years. They were so close that they called each other colorful names without offense. Micaela introduced Gloria to Brenda, another friend of hers, and the 3 of them started hanging out. During their second outing, Brenda wanted to be accepted and liked by Gloria so she referred to Gloria with the colorful names that Micaela did. Gloria didn't like someone she just met being that familiar with her, especially that soon. So she had a conversation with Brenda and set limits with her.

Who: *Brenda (any new acquaintance)*
What: *Calling her colorful names, inappropriate familiarity*
When: *Any time*
Where: *Anywhere*
How long: *Until consent is granted*

SUMMARY

When you understand that boundaries are contextual, you will then empower yourself to make the most appropriate real-time choices regarding your life and health. The *Who, What, When, Where,* and *How long* nature of healthy boundaries provides you with the flexibility of limiting your exposure to harmful people and situations.

Contextualizing Your Boundaries Activity

1. Think of the 10 people you spend the most time with who are not children you're currently raising. The 10 may be family

members, friends, coworkers, classmates, business associates, instructors, retailers, etc.

What seats do they currently occupy in your life? Add their names next to the theatre sections below:

Backstage   _____

Front row   _____

Orchestra   _____

Mezzanine   _____

Balcony   _____

Lobby   _____

Box office   _____

Parking lot   _____

2. With your new understanding of boundary context, are there any seats you want to reassign? If yes, then revise your seating chart below and note any applicable context:

Backstage   _____

Front row   _____

Orchestra   _____

Mezzanine   _____

Balcony   _____

Lobby   _____

Box office   _____

Parking lot   _____

What changed for you?

_____

_____

CHAPTER 11

LIVING MINDFULLY

*"Mindfulness is simply being aware of what is
happening right now..."*
—James Baraz

In order to be conscious of your boundaries, potential violations, and red flags in real time, present moment awareness is required. You see, being present is to be fully aware of what you think, feel, and do at any given moment. It also includes an alertness to activities about and around you. This is also called mindfulness. What does this have to do with healthy boundaries? Let me explain.

Recall Edith and Josh from the physical boundary example in Chapter 3 with him reacting to Edith's hug. Josh's shoulders hunched when she, whom he wasn't close to, hugged him because Josh was present and attuned to his intuition. In real time, he recognized that Edith's hug was inappropriate and was able to act immediately to protect his space by keeping his hands at his sides during the hug and then by backing away from her.

Had Josh not been present or attuned to his intuition, he would have missed the red flag of the inappropriate hug, would not have protected his personal space, and would have given the false impression that it was okay for Edith to hug him without his knowledge or consent.

In another example, think of hurriedly leaving the grocery store with bags. The person hanging around the parking lot eases very close to you. Your intuition alerts you with a creepy feeling that skirts your skin, with the knot in your belly, or with the hairs on the back of your neck that suddenly stand. These sensations occur in real time, in the moment. And if you're not present and paying attention because you're worried about getting home late and having dinner ready on time for your boyfriend and making him mad and then have to hear him tell you how worthless you are, then you will not react to any threats to your person and will not be able to protect yourself like maintaining distance from that person or going back into the store to request an escort to your car.

Being present enables you to recognize what is happening within and around you as it is occurring. While your awareness is heightened, it is not chaotic nor is it negative nervous energy. Mindfulness is seemingly a paradox—acute awareness of everything and nothing simultaneously. So you can focus on paying for your groceries while being alert enough to respond to any nearby dangers and potential boundary violations.

Presence and mindfulness can also be experienced as laser focus, being absorbed by a single topic or task like sewing or yoga. Thoughts about dinner, work, or weight pull you out of the present moment and can cause injury. I loved to sew because it was very meditative to me. The pinpoint focus required to create accurate seams and not sew my fingers was so relaxing. I had no worries or problems when I sewed, there was no past or future, and not to mention that creating something was very rewarding. And yoga…the mindfulness necessary to perform the poses and make adjustments without hurting myself is gratifying on multiple levels.

Anxiety

When you are not present, your mind is either in the future, the past, or blank. Neither is aligned with reality and is laced with distorted thoughts, which are discussed further in the next chapter, Thinking Distortions and Boundaries. Anxiety is future-oriented gloom and doom thinking. It foreshadows frightening events and outcomes.

Your mind is then absorbed with finding a way to control the future because anxiety convinces you that you must know all the answers, fix all the problems, do so now, and make sure it all works out.

That's a lot. And it's unrealistic. We humans do not have the capacity to know everything. We don't have the ability to fix everything. And we have zero control over the future. Anxiety is a setup for failure because it focuses you on things you can't control while taking your attention away from the only control you have, which is in the here-and-now.

> *"If you want to conquer the anxiety of life, live in the moment, live in the breath."*
> —Amit Ray

Depression

Depression is dwelling on the past, which presents as *why did that happen to me?* or *why can't things be the way they were?* Thus, your energy is spent trying to find a way to change what has already occurred so you can stop the self-loathing, stop feeling unloved, or stop blaming yourself for what happened and erase the negative self-identity you created when the bad thing happened.

Similar to anxiety, we humans cannot time travel to control the future or to change the past. Healing is a present-moment process. While it involves addressing past experiences, healing is dealing with them in the here-and-now. The best we humans can do with the past is to honestly reflect on the facts of what happened, not the negative imprint you imposed upon yourself when it was happening. Use that information to make the best decisions now and that will positively influence your future.

We will take a deeper look at anxiety, depression, and emotions in Chapter 15, Living Boundaries and Mental Health. For now, know that being present and living mindfully are major factors in mental, emotional, and overall health and well-being.

> *"Research tells us that when you live in the moment—that is, getting out of your head and being consciously aware of your surroundings—you will usually feel happier and experience less stress."*
> —TherapistAid.com

Living Mindfully Strategies

Below are my top 5 favorite tools for living mindfully.

1. Movement

Physical movement is one of the best ways to shift your emotional experience. Moving your body, as described in *Living In Total Health,* is more than exercise. You can think of movement as activity—organized and systematic ways of using the body in space. Movement includes tennis, dancing, swimming, reorganizing the garage, walking, hiking, yoga, biking, or any athletic endeavor.

Also note that physical movement burns off negative excess energy, redirects your attention in a positive direction, and releases endorphins—feel good hormones we humans naturally make that can alleviate pain, lower stress, improve mood, and enhance your sense of well-being.

Movement promotes mindfulness.

2. Meditation

Many clients remark that mediation doesn't work for them because they don't stop thinking to achieve a 'blank' mind. My response to them is that mediation is not about a blank mind. Rather, meditation is about not attaching to what is in your mind. Attaching to thoughts also involves applying emotional energy to them which results in judging the thoughts themselves and criticizing yourself for having them. Allowing thoughts to flow in and out of awareness without attachment or judgement, for me, is meditation. Remaining at peace with detachment from thoughts is mindful.

Meditation promotes mindfulness.

3. **Yoga**

As physical movement and meditation promote present-moment-awareness, so does yoga. This activity integrates movement with mindfulness and includes the benefits of burning off negative excess energy, increasing muscle tone and flexibility, redirecting attention in a healthy way, releasing endorphins, and mental detachment from stress.

Yoga is physical and mindful.

4. **Stress Less Box**

The Stress Less Box is a unique tool I designed to enhance mindfulness and mental flexibility, thereby reducing and possibly eliminating the distorted and unrealistic thinking inherent in anxiety and depression. Most clients who have experienced the Stress Less Box reported that while using it to ground, they were not aware of any anxiety, depression, or stressors. Their focus was only on the visual cues the box provided.

The Stress Less Box promotes grounding, presence, and seeing new insights and possibilities.

5. Journaling

Journal Therapy is a very effective way to live mindfully because it has been shown to reduce anxiety, depression, stress, and improve the immune system. Also known as expressive writing, journaling is a healthy outlet for your deepest thoughts, feelings, and experiences without judgement.

Journaling enhances your mental and overall health and well-being.

SUMMARY

Being present and experiencing life in real time is empowering because your awareness provides optimal access to your choices, including recognizing red flags in real time. Living in the future with anxiety or in the past with depression robs you of your inherent personal power to protect and to nurture yourself. Thus, utilizing the above tools can promote mindfulness, improve your mental health, overall well-being, and safety.

Living Mindfully Activity:

1. How mindful are you right now? Scan your mind and body then answer the following questions:
   - What are you thinking?

   _____

   - What are you doing?

   _____

   - What do you feel? (physical sensations)

   _____

2. What mindful tools do you engage in? Check all that apply and circle how often you engage.

☐ Movement – daily weekly monthly annually never

☐ Meditation – daily weekly monthly annually never

☐ Yoga – daily weekly monthly annually never

☐ Stress Less Box – daily weekly monthly annually never

☐ Journaling – daily weekly monthly annually never

☐ Other

CHAPTER 12

THINKING DISTORTIONS AND BOUNDARIES

"The primary cause of unhappiness is never the situation, but your thoughts about it. Be aware of the thoughts you are thinking."
—Eckhart Tolle

Humans are blessed with the ability to think and reason. This mental gift is a major aspect of the incredibleness of humanity and mental health. Thoughts are a tool to help us organize and decipher life experiences, and they are automatic. These automatic thoughts tend to be based upon negative life experience and the negativity learned from parents and other influential people.

Unfortunately, however, some people don't go beyond the inaccurate initial and automatic interpretations of life formed as negative thoughts and assume they accurately reflect reality. Please know that thoughts are not facts, nor are they an accurate reflection of reality in and of themselves. Such unrealistic thoughts are called Cognitive Distortions. As the name suggests, these thoughts twist reality to fit beliefs rather than the human adjusting their beliefs to align with reality. Doing so would make living life more fluid.

Dr. David D. Burns in *The Feeling Good Handbook* popularized the concept of distorted thinking and described 10 types of distorted thinking patterns. Cognitive Distortions are also known as thinking errors and automatic appraisals. Below are the most common Cognitive Distortions that my clients present in therapy.

1. **All or Nothing:**

    You only see 2 polar opposites—black/white, good/bad, always/never, win/lose. There is no middle or gray area. Life is either one extreme or automatically the other and all other possibilities are overlooked.

    Kelly complained that his anxiety wasn't better because he still worried a lot, ignoring the progress he made, which included his panic attacks ceased and he drove again confidently.

2. **Overgeneralization:**

    You see one negative event or person as an accurate representation of all with the same traits.

    Bailey encounters a rude cashier, then thinks every cashier is rude. Typical terms of overgeneralization include they are, all of them, those people. Examples: *"All men lie". "Those people from X city are lazy". "They're all ignorant in country X".*

3. **Mental Filter / Perfectionism:**

    You dwell on one negative or minor detail with laser-like focus then deem your entire effort a failure. You reject normal human error and learning.

    Dana planned and hosted an event. There weren't enough seats for those who didn't RSVP, which was the only detail he didn't plan for. Dana was mortified and berated himself for failing to accommodate everyone, ignoring the positive feedback he did receive from guests.

4. **Disqualifying the Positive:**

You dismiss positive experiences and compliments to maintain negative beliefs about yourself and life. When someone says something positive about you, you find something wrong with that person and their judgment to dismiss their compliment.

Pat's boss thanked her for completing monthly reports on time. She responded, "That's what I'm supposed to do."

5. **Jumping to Conclusions:**

You assume to know the bad things that will happen. You fortune-tell gloom and doom. You read other people's minds for their negative thoughts about you.

It's August and Kelly is already anxious about Thanksgiving because she assumes her mean uncle will be there and then she'll have to play nice when he insults her as he usually does.

6. **Magnification / Catastrophizing:**

Extreme exaggeration that blows a usually minor adverse event out of proportion. Drama Queen/Drama King.

A new coworker is shy, so she is quiet and reserved in the breakroom. You take it to mean that she doesn't like you. And because she doesn't like you, she'll talk bad about you to the boss which will result in you getting demoted or fired.

> ➢ **Minimization** is basically the opposite— downplaying the significance or seriousness of an emotion or experience. Dismissing the reality of what's actually happening invalidates you and undermines your confidence, esteem, and worth. Minimization also robs you of the chance to set

boundaries, problem solve, and make needed adjustments.

> Pat's father missed another tennis match, this time a championship. Pat responded, "It's no big deal."

7. Emotional Reasoning:

You believe how you *feel* = reality and make choices based on impulse, rather than the best option available. You allow your emotions to control you instead of learning from them.

An abuser hits his wife because he feels anger. A lonely woman doesn't socialize because she feels anxiety. A woman calls her ex a lot because she feels sad about the breakup. In reality, life moves forward no matter how you "feel". Thus, emotional reasoning causes you to lose time and credibility.

8. Should Statements:

You use guilt and shame for motivation and tell yourself you should, must, need to, have to, got to, and ought to.

You've internalized the standards and expectations of how other people want you to be and what to do, which sets you up for failure. These statements destroy your choices by imposing others' needs and desires on you. Examples are "I should be successful by now", "I have to stop doing that", and "I ought to lose weight".

9. Labeling / Mislabeling:

You apply a negative and permanent characteristic to yourself or another person, which fails to describe the behavior you want to change.

Examples include: I am weak. You are lazy. She is stupid. He is a loser. Bailey's son played video games after school instead of doing homework. He told his son, "You're a dumb boy" instead of addressing his son's choice and helping him learn how to prioritize.

10. Personalization:

You take blame for negative events and the consequences of other people's choices that aren't your responsibility, believing you have control over another person's experience. Personalization also involves giving in and agreeing to something you don't want or are uncomfortable with just to be liked or keep someone from being angry with you.

A battered woman blames herself for her abuser's violence. A father feels guilty for his adult son's bankruptcy. A mother blames herself for her daughter's infertility.

"People-pleasing trades boundaries and authenticity for temporary and misguided scraps of self-worth."
—Albert Bramante, PhD, Talent Agent, Author

Note that distortions are intensified when combined with others: *I'm so stupid, I should know this by now. Forgot to buy ice when I went grocery shopping...I always forget, I'm a loser.*

Distorted thinking is harmful physically, mentally, emotionally, and spiritually because it inhibits your ability to identify, set, and maintain appropriate boundaries.

Jorden was proud of being a productive employee. She knew her manager relied on her to get things done with the time and tools she needed to complete tasks. Recently, however, a few staff members were laid off, which increased Jorden's workload to the point where she could not complete all of her duties. Even still, she continued to take on new tasks whenever her manager asked, no matter what she already had on her plate that day. And when the manager thanked Jorden for her hard work, she thought the manager only said that in order to give her more work to do. Within 3 months, Jorden went home exhausted and angry, which strained her marriage and led her to detest going to work.

Jorden presented with anger and depression in therapy. She was angry with herself because she *should* be able to get it all done each work day. Jorden called herself a failure when she could not complete a few non-urgent tasks in one shift. In discussing her asking for assistance, prioritizing her workload, setting realistic goals, taking breaks, accepting compliments, setting limits on new tasks she agreed to, and being kinder to herself, Jorden recognized her distorted thinking and how it negatively impacted her. She learned to catch those thoughts, reframe them, and set appropriate boundaries for herself at work. Jorden's anger and depression resolved, she enjoyed her work again, and her home life improved too because she was in a better mood after work.

Poor Boundaries:

> Jorden saying 'yes' to new tasks when already overloaded (Should Statements).
> Jorden saying 'yes' because she didn't want to let her manager down (Personalization).
> Jorden 'Shoulding' herself to be perfect and complete all tasks during her shift (Should Statements, Mental Filter, All or Nothing).
> Jorden seeing herself as a failure (Labeling).
> Jorden dismissing her manager's compliment (Disqualifying the Positive).

Healthy Boundaries:

✓ Jorden setting realistic goals for what she could accomplish during her shift.

- ✓ Jorden accepting her manager's compliments about her hard work.
- ✓ Jorden asking her manager for assistance.
- ✓ Jorden managing her mood and emotions so work didn't impact home.
- ✓ Jorden reframing her distorted thoughts.

When it comes to distorted thinking, it is the thought that counts. When you ignore, overlook, or dismiss reality, you chip away at your self-confidence and self-worth, and trigger anxiety, depression or both. Reality does not bend to fit my twisted thoughts nor yours. The best you or I can do is accept the truth of things as they are and cope from there.

Please understand that thoughts are not facts. Just because a thought occurs does not mean it's true, accurate, or even realistic. And just as important, thoughts are transient events. Left alone, they pass quickly through our consciousness. It's when we attach to or judge them as good or bad, true or false, that reality gets skewed.

Acknowledging and accepting reality is step 1. Next comes challenging the automatic distortions then reframing your thoughts to reflect reality, which will enable you to cope better, improve your boundaries, and enhance your life experience.

CHAPTER 13

AFFIRMING YOUR BOUNDARIES

*"Boundaries need to be communicated first verbally
and then with actions."*
—Henry Cloud

Setting and maintaining boundaries is crucial for your health and wellness. Affirming your boundaries involves all of the elements previously discussed. Knowing that boundaries are your innate alarm system, identifying your deal breakers, understanding healthy versus unhealthy boundaries, seeing red flags in real time, understanding the contextual nature of boundaries, accepting the truths about boundaries, being present, and accepting reality together strengthen your ability to nurture and protect yourself.

The process of affirming your boundaries begins with my *ICAN,* which is outlined below. I developed *ICAN* to simplify the how-to of affirming your boundaries. Examples that include how these steps relate to the boundary truths in Chapter 9 are provided.

I*dentify* your lines in the sand.
The first step in affirming your boundaries is identifying what they are and include your deal breakers from Chapter 4. Make a list of your top 5 boundaries that you want to set with others using the form at the end of this chapter. Consider every area of your life: significant other, family, friends, work, etc., and *who, what, when, where, how long.* Once you have your list of boundaries to set, then select the easiest place to start for practice and to build your confidence.

C*ommunicate* your line in the sand verbally.

It's imperative to communicate the boundaries you've identified with other people so they are informed about where you stand. Guessing or hoping that they "get it" is unrealistic and leaves you vulnerable to manipulation, abuse, and other forms of harm. So, your initial communication is *verbalizing*, using your words, to convey where your line in the sand is and to give others the opportunity to adjust to your boundaries. It is important to be clear in your communication to avoid passive and vague language.

Boundary Truth #1: *Humans will continue to do what they're allowed to get away with.*

Communicating your boundaries is only the beginning of putting others on notice as to what you will or will not allow them to get away with.

A*pply* consequences with action.

Remember Boundary Truth #4 from Chapter 9? *No* is not enough. That Truth applies here, where you behave your boundaries. The previous step of communication involved speaking words to denote your boundaries. Taking action and behaving your boundaries are deeper and more effective ways to communicate and are required when words don't successfully convey your line in the sand. Too many people skip this step because they hope that saying *"no"* is enough and that their work is then done. However, this step demonstrates the saying, *"Action speaks louder than words."*

Boundary Truth #2: *Human behavior unchecked escalates. It gets worse.*

The absence of consequences and the presence of ineffective ones incentivize the person with the inappropriate behavior to continue it. Therefore, applying consequences alerts the boundary violator that their actions are unacceptable to you.

N*avigate* your choices and your consequences.

The choices you make in regards to setting and affirming your boundaries do have consequences. In fact, each choice we humans make yields either a positive, negative, or neutral consequence. Note that *yes* to one thing is *no* to another, and vice-versa. So it is a matter of which consequence you can live with that minimizes any potential negative emotional experiences that you may have. It is important to know that many people skip this step too because they desire a perfect outcome, meaning that they hope there will be no pushback from setting and affirming their boundaries.

Many anxious clients mistakenly believe that the "right" choice only has positive consequences. So they overthink how to make their decisions turn out well for everyone involved, which is impossible and increases their anxiety. Be aware that this step also involves the context and Boundary Truth #3—how you manage your boundaries teaches other people how to treat you. If there are no consequences or effective ones for violating your boundaries, then your boundaries will be violated again.

Thus, navigating your boundaries involves how you apply the consequences to those who violate, i.e., what actions you take to enforce the limits you set on others to protect and nurture yourself. Do you say *no* ad nauseum? Do you bite your tongue and hope they get it? Do you leave the situation, end the relationship, or distance yourself from the trespasser? Many clients jump to conclusions and personalize following through on consequences. So at this point, it is very important to be aware of and reframe your distorted thoughts because they will hinder how you apply your consequences and take action.

Boundary Truth #4: N*o is not enough. You must behave your boundaries.*

And keep in mind that affirming your boundaries is necessary because most people do not self-correct. They typically don't figure out on their own that their behavior is harmful to you. Even if they do figure it out, there's no incentive for them to change when they can get what they want from you with their same behaviors. So it is your responsibility to affirm your boundaries. Therefore, consequences, positive and negative, put others on notice about what you will and will not tolerate.

Boundary Truth #5: You are already empowered to protect and to nurture yourself.

Below are examples of how ICAN plays out in real life.

Example 1

Genie grew tired of people taking advantage of her. She realized that she gave in to the excessive and sometimes unreasonable demands of family, friends, and coworkers. Genie even acknowledged that she gave money to homeless individuals every time they asked. This behavior ran up her credit card balances because she gave her cash away and was forced to buy food and gas on credit. She could not afford to continue giving money so freely, so she started there. While saying "no" to a homeless person triggered her guilt, it did not bring the fears of disapproval that saying "no" to a loved one did.

Genie established a monthly "budget" for donations to the homeless, her line in the sand. Next, she practiced verbalizing "no" to requests for money that totaled more than her budget allowed her to spend. And because Genie did not encounter the same homeless individuals on a regular basis, no real consequences were necessary. She simply gave money she allotted for or she communicated "no" when she couldn't.

I: Genie wants to limit how much money she gives to strangers.

C: *Sorry, I don't have cash* or *Sorry, I don't have money to spare.*

A: Keep walking, keep her purse closed.

N: Genie felt guilty yet was proud of herself for not giving in and staying within her budget, her commitment to herself.

Example 2

I partnered with Roland for a business project. There were no personal discussions about relationships, sex, or the like. After we completed the project, Roland and I celebrated at lunch. A few nights later, my phone rang at about 1:00 am. It was Roland. Thinking it was an emergency, I answered by asking, *"Are you okay?"* He replied, *"Yeah. Just called to see how you're doing."* I replied, *"I was asleep. Goodnight."* and hung up the phone.

Roland called about the same time again a couple of nights later. And again, it was not an emergency. My final comment before hanging up was, *"Please don't call me after 9pm."*

When he called again in the wee hours, I did not answer and blocked his number. Whatever he wanted was not what I wanted and crossed my line in the sand—I did not tolerate late night non-emergent telephone calls.

I: Stop receiving non-emergent late night calls from business associates.

C: *Please don't call me after 9pm.*

A: Hang up, don't answer, block number.

N: Accept the potential consequence of losing a business partner to affirm my boundaries.

Note that in example 2 above regarding the business associate, each communication with him to set the boundary for appropriate calling times intensified. The consequence became more and more severe—from hanging up the phone, to not answering his call, to then blocking his number. Because people continue to do what they're allowed to get away with, Boundary Truth #1, most will push back when you begin setting boundaries with them so a graduated escalation of the consequences may be necessary.

Example 3

Recall the example of withholding and punishment from chapter 6. Mary punishes her partner Sarina for disagreeing with her about various aspects of their relationship—money, family, entertainment, etc. Sarina wants to voice her opinion without Mary giving her the cold shoulder.

I: Sarina be able to express her opinion and disagree without getting punished.
C: *I get angry when you shut me out for expressing myself; I need to share my opinion about our life together.*
A: Speak up for herself and self-advocate.
N: Sarina accepts the potential consequence of breaking up with Mary if she doesn't respect or accept her opinions and input.

Example 4

A client named Rochelle was frustrated with her pre-teen son and daughter. They rarely did their chores and ignored her when she reminded them to. Rochelle did not enjoy yelling at and nagging them to fulfill their responsibilities. So, she set appropriate boundaries with them.

I: Son and daughter complete chores without multiple promptings.
C: *Your chores are...pick up the trash in your rooms and put your dirty clothes in the hamper every day before play time, and put your trash in the bin outside for pickup.*

A: If you don't do your chores, then you will lose a privilege for a week.

N: Accept the potential consequence of rebellion and attitude from her children, and cope with guilt that may arise for enforcing her rules.

Example 5

When I meet with a new client in the intake sessions, I explain my approach to therapy and the importance of developing and strengthening coping skills. Recently during intake, this client stated that she wanted therapy based on a specific psychological theory after my spiel. I replied that that particular theory is not my area of expertise and she was welcome to request a therapist who practices XYZ theory. The client then asked me, *"Well, can you look it up? It's not that complicated."*

I: Me focusing on my area of expertise and not spending time learning another theory to please this client.

C: *No, I won't do that.* (I said this softly) *There are many other therapists who are already versed in that theory.*

A: Provide therapy from my professional expertise if she chose to continue working with me.

N: Accept the potential consequence of the client getting angry with me and possibly complaining about me.

Example 6

Early on in our marriage, my first husband committed me to events and activities whenever he was asked to by his family members and friends without asking me first. This put me in the position of canceling my plans, not making plans, or not attending functions. Although I was willing to say "no" at appropriate times, I didn't like either option I was presented with nor did I enjoy being put in that position by him. So, I had a conversation with him about it.

I: Me choosing which events and activities I engaged in, rather than my husband committing me without asking me first.

C: *Please ask me if I'm interested in going to functions before you commit me to them.*

A: I declined to attend functions if he committed me without asking about my interest, and if I had other plans.

N: Accept and understand that he may be disappointed in or angry with me for declining to attend the events he committed me to.

SUMMARY

Communicating your line in the sand gives your loved ones and others the opportunity to adjust by respecting your boundaries. In this case, my first husband did adjust and stopped committing me to events without my consent. Subsequently, in applying consequences and navigation, I thanked him for refraining from committing me to events and activities without asking me first. Positive consequences work too.

Affirming Your Boundaries Activity

Building upon your new knowledge about boundary basics, red flags, and the truths about boundaries, the next step is to verbally communicate your boundaries to others. Use the worksheet below to practice communicating your boundaries verbally—spoken, with words. Then use your words to develop your own ICAN.

1. Make a list of the top 5 boundaries that you want to set with others. You can always add additional boundaries as they occur to you, though 5 is a good place to start.

Boundary #1_____ Who:_____

Boundary #2_____ Who:_____

Boundary #3_____ Who:_____

Boundary #4_____ Who:_____

Boundary #5_____ Who:_____

2. Practice the phrases below or use them to develop your own ways to speak the boundaries you noted above. Keep in mind that with effective communication less is more. Takers and abusers look for loopholes in your verbiage to use against you and gain the advantage. Say the phrases below out loud and in front of a mirror. The more you rehearse them, then the more comfortable you'll be speaking them to others.

➤ No.
➤ Not at this time.
➤ I'm not comfortable with...
➤ Please don't call or text after 9 pm.
➤ I'm not interested.
➤ No thank you.
➤ I don't want to...
➤ I need time to think about it.
➤ I'm not available.
➤ Other statements you can make to communicate "no".

_____

_____

_____

3. Describe a recent situation in which your boundaries were violated.

_____

_____

_____

_____

_____

4. Use ICAN for the situation above:

    Identify the boundary involved

    _____

    Communicate your line in the sand verbally

    _____

    Apply consequences

    _____

    Navigate your choices and consequences. What will you do if you receive pushback?

    _____

    _____

    _____

    _____

    _____

    _____

CHAPTER 14

COMMUNICATING YOUR BOUNDARIES NON-VERBALLY

"No is not enough. You must behave your boundaries."
—Glen Alex

In Chapter 13, Affirming Your Boundaries, you learned the ICAN method of managing your boundaries. ICAN included verbal communication, actually saying what your line in the sand is. Speaking your boundaries is the first step in affirming them to others. Using your words garners a worthy level of attention from those with whom you speak.

However, effective communication involves more than verbalization. Behavior is a great way to get your message across to another person because some people ignore what is said. They weather the storm of your words, so to speak, and look for spaces between your utterances to insert themselves and get what they want from you. This reflects the saying *"Action speaks louder than words."* and is why Boundary Truth #4 is true – *"no"* is not enough.

When others ignore your verbal communications of your line in the sand, you must behave your boundaries. Recall Ashley Judd from the Understanding the Truths about Boundaries chapter. She behaved her repeated *no* to the producer who ignored her by walking out of their meeting.

While words communicate verbally, non-verbal aspects of communication convey messages emotionally. We humans are emotional creatures. Many decisions people make are based upon how they *feel* and what they want rather than reason and the intellect. Marketers are well aware of this and create ads that appeal to emotions instead of logic. For example, it's been said that stock market crashes result from the investors' fear, an emotion, leading them to sell off their stock suddenly and impulsively.

> *"Understanding investors' mindsets and behaviors is an interesting and integral part of studying the stock market. Investors are often driven by emotions like fear and greed, which can lead to market anomalies and inefficiencies."*
> —Professor Krupa Desai, Southern New Hampshire University

Non-verbal communication can be far more influential than speaking words because body language encompasses emotions and intentions. Non-verbal cues include eye contact, facial expressions, posture, gestures, and behavior. Below is a brief overview of each body language element.

Eye Contact

Looking directly into someone's eyes shows your confidence, authenticity, and sincerity. Conversely, looking away, shifting or roving eyes indicate a person is being dishonest and possibly fabricating what they say. And rapidly blinking eyes can convey discomfort and vulnerability. This non-verbal cue allows you to demonstrate that you mean what you say and enables you to discern how credible another person is.

Facial Expressions

This element of body language reveals your emotional reactions, which are based upon your thoughts and interpretations. A smile typically indicates joy, pleasure, or excitement. Frowning denotes displeasure, maybe even sadness or anger. A smirk sends the message of ridicule and not taking someone seriously. Raised eyebrows can indicate surprise while one raised eyebrow reflects a question, curiosity, or suspicion.

Posture

How you position and carry your body relates whether you are open, closed, friendly, hostile, or anxious. Your posture tells how confident and secure you are when standing tall with shoulders back and down. Hunched and rounded shoulders indicate uncertainty and insecurity. Crossed arms say "I'm closed" to what's being said, new ideas, suggestions, and the like.

Gestures

While posture is about the position of your whole body, gestures are the position and movement of individual body parts. Gestures include thumbs up, the okay sign with the fingers, nodding or tilting the head, patting or pointing to the heart area in the chest, thumbs down, hunching the shoulders, shaking the head yes or no, clinched fist, and finger pointing. Your gestures send messages of agreement, disagreement, interest, excitement, joy, love, anxiety, anger, etc.

Behavior

Your behavior may be the most expressive form of non-verbal cues. Again action, what you do, is the combination of your thoughts, emotions, intentions, and desires in motion. So, behavior communicates a lot of information about you. Facing someone and looking at them, leaning forward, shaking hands, and appropriate touching express interest, concern, joy. In contrast, fidgeting, shifting body weight, standing sideways, moving around, looking at your phone or TV or computer, yawning, backing up, getting too close, and turning away convey disrespect, disinterest, boredom, anxiety.

SUMMARY

Be aware that the non-verbal communication signals discussed above may vary from culture to culture and context. Also understand that while dishonest people may say the 'right' words, those can be incongruent with their non-verbal messages. So when the words and behavior don't match, believe the behavior because it is the expression of that person's thoughts, intentions, desires, and emotions.

The non-verbal cues, what you show rather than say, matter just as much if not more than words when it comes to communicating your boundaries to other people. Your eye contact, facial expressions, gestures, posture, and behavior all speak volumes on the emotional level. In order to effectively communicate your line in the sand, these cues must match your spoken words to maximize you being taken seriously and being understood.

For example, Katrina gets frustrated when her husband cuts her off while they converse and changes the topic often. She finally decided to speak up for herself after 18 months. Her opportunity to do so came at dinner. Sitting across the table from him, they talked about their next vacation. As Katrina was sharing where she wanted to go, he interrupted her and started talking about his job.

"I wish you would stop cutting me off.", she snapped while looking down at her plate, twirling the fork in her food, shoulders slumped. Katrina's husband ignored her and kept talking about work.

COMMUNICATION WORKSHEET

*"Healthy relationships thrive on clear boundaries
and open communication."*
—Unknown

Building upon your new knowledge about boundary basics, green and red flags, truths, and intuition, use the worksheet below to create a template for how you can best communicate your line in the sand to others so they can be clear about what you will and won't tolerate. Identify your verbal and non-verbal forms of communication.

Let's use the example from the previous chapter, Communicating Your Boundaries Non-Verbally:

> *Katrina gets frustrated when her husband interrupts her while she speaks. She snapped at him with slumped shoulders while looking down at her plate and twirling the fork in her food.*

Verbal

Write down variations of the phrases below or use them to develop your own ways to speak your boundaries then practice saying them to become more comfortable verbalizing your line in the sand. Keep in mind that with effective communication less is more because takers and abusers look for loopholes in your verbiage to use against you and gain the advantage.

Stop cutting me off. <u>I'd appreciate you letting me finish. Please don't interrupt me.</u>

I don't like when...

_____

Stop interrupting me…

_____

I'm not okay with...

_____

Let me finish…

_____

Non-verbal

Body language is non-verbal communication and it must match your words. Eye contact, posture, facial expression, gestures, and behavior are important forms of communication just as important as speaking words. If your body language is different from what you say, then your words will not be heard and you won't be taken seriously.

Katrina: looked down and twirled her fork with slumped shoulders.

How can Katrina improve her non-verbal signals? Fill in the blanks.

Eye contact:

_____

Facial expressions:

_____

Posture:

_____

Gestures:

_____

Behavior:

_____

Do your non-verbal cues match your words?

□ Yes   □ No   □ Need improvement

What improvements can you make?

Eye contact:

_____

Facial expressions:

_____

Posture:

_____

Gestures:

_____

Behavior:

_____

CHAPTER 15

LIVING BOUNDARIES AND MENTAL HEALTH

*"Boundaries are essential because they can improve
your overall health and well-being."*
—Sarah Barkley

Let's talk about mental health. As the foundation for health and happiness, healthy boundaries minimize exposure to harm, strengthen your resolve and resilience, and repel anxiety, depression, and stress. Healthy boundaries enable you to successfully navigate through life's challenges to experience authentic love and joy as safely as possible.

How exactly do boundaries improve mental health? Keep reading to learn how healthy boundaries reduce anxiety, alleviate depression, relieve stress, and enable you to engage in emotional intelligence to enhance your mental wellness.

REDUCING ANXIETY

According to the Centers for Disease Control (CDC), anxiety is the number one mental health disorder among American adults. As described in the Living Mindfully chapter, anxiety is future-oriented gloom and doom thinking. Anxious thinking can consume and overwhelm you, and often leads to panic attacks. Overthinking, constant worry, anticipating the negative, jumping to conclusions, nervous energy, fidgeting, feeling on edge, and fearing bad things happening are common presentations of anxiety.

Anxiety tricks you into believing that you must have all the answers, fix all the problems, do so now, and guarantee a successful outcome. That's a lot. And it's all unrealistic. We human beings do not have the capacity to know everything nor do we have the ability to fix everything. And we certainly have no control over the future and over other people. Thus, the failure isn't being unable to exercise that control. The failure is in trying to do so.

Anxiety is predicated on unrealistic control. Some clients have communicated to me that if they think hard enough, then they can figure out how to keep bad things from happening, prepare for those bad things, and think (overthink) how to ensure positive results, including what other people think of them. Other clients have said that they attempt to think of ways to keep other people from being mean or harmful to them by guessing and anticipating what those other people will do to preempt it. Such are attempts to control the uncontrollable, which trigger and exacerbate anxiety.

If you ask me to fly a plane or drive a semi-truck, then I will fail. Both are unrealistic for me because I don't have the necessary skillsets to pilot an airplane or drive a semi, nor the desire to learn them. So judging yourself negatively because of the lack of skills, to grieve for example, or desire is the same as telling yourself that you *should* be/have/do this. It is an unrealistic expectation based upon irrational thinking patterns, i.e., cognitive distortions, and they set you up for failure. In addition, anxiety keeps you steeped in the unrealistic, stuck, and paralyzed.

The Thinking Well chapter in *Living In Total Health* describes 10 distorted thinking patterns because they trigger or exacerbate anxiety and depression, having a significant impact on mental and total health. In this book, the Thinking Distortions and Boundaries chapter connect distorted thinking patterns to boundary issues.

The Anxiety and Depression Association of America reported that anxiety disorders "are highly treatable". Identifying your personal realm of control empowers you and effectively reduces anxiety. Let's look at two examples.

Example 1

As an apprentice in construction, Randy experienced a lot of anxiety because of his boss' angry outbursts. In unpacking Randy's experience, he revealed that he was on hyper alert to stop his boss' reactions and behavior. That is, Randy sought to control his boss' reactions and behavior. Because of this, Randy experienced nervous energy, excessive worry, fear of disapproval, and feeling on edge at work. Every move he made was an attempt to preempt his boss' feelings, emotions, and reactions.

In therapy, Randy finally realized that he had no control over his boss' experience, which is an emotional boundary issue. The Boundaries Chapter in *Living In Total Health* discusses emotional boundaries as does the *Categorizing Your Boundaries* chapter of this book. While Randy was responsible for what he personally said and did, he was not responsible for how anyone, including his boss, responded to him.

Randy was then able to recognize his realm of control and separate his boss' experience from his own. This understanding enabled him to accept that his boss' outbursts were his own issues and not about Randy's worth as a human being. So Randy stopped trying to preempt and control his boss' reactions. In doing so, Randy was able to be more efficient by focusing on his work instead of his worry. Randy also improved his emotional boundaries utilizing the coping tools he learned in therapy to reduce his anxiety at work.

Example 2

Katrina started therapy with the goal to learn how to change her family members so they would respect her and do what she wanted them to do for her without her having to ask. Yet, she was unwilling to set and affirm appropriate boundaries with any of them. Katrina was *overwhelmed* (the term she regularly used to describe her experience) working full time, managing her chronic medical condition, caring for her elderly parents, and doing everything for her adult children and siblings, even though they were fully capable of doing the things like grocery shopping and making travel arrangements for themselves. Instead of setting appropriate limits with them to save space to take good care of herself, Katrina continued to say *yes*, adding more and more to her plate.

Katrina's *overwhelm* was actually anxiety. Note here that overwhelm and stress are other ways to describe anxiety, the experience of being out of control. She worried about how to please her family members constantly, hoping they would automatically reciprocate. Katrina stayed on edge in fear that if she set appropriate limits with her family members then she would not receive their love or approval. Katrina resisted the fact that she could not control other human beings, that she was only responsible for and in control of her own actions. Thus, she refused to exercise her realistic control in setting and maintaining appropriate boundaries with others.

Katrina did not work to improve her mental or emotional boundaries with family members. Therefore, her quest to change family members to meet her needs was unsuccessful. Successful navigation through stress, overwhelm, and anxiety is predicated on healthy boundaries.

"Having solid boundaries can decrease stress, increase self-esteem, and create comfortable social interactions."
—Masterclass

ALLEVIATING DEPRESSION

Depression is the second most prevalent mental health disorder that is experienced by American adults, according to the CDC. This mental health issue is predicated on the past. The Living Mindfully chapter discusses how clients who experience depression dwell on the past in terms of *why did that happen to me?* or *why can't things be the way they were?*

Depression can be triggered by the death of your loved one, divorce or breakup, job or financial loss, empty nest, chronic anxiety and stress, your best friend moving away, leaving one home for another one, trauma, abuse, or some other major life change. These triggers are examples of loss. So you can think of depression as the evolution of unresolved grief, which is the process of releasing the mental and emotional attachment to that which is no longer present in your life. Sadness is the emotion through which grief expresses itself.

Similar to anxiety, depression tends to create or exacerbate tunnel vision. That is, narrow-minded and limited thinking are predominant. Depression significantly inhibits your ability to perceive realistic options available to you in the present and it restricts your acceptance of what is already valuable in your life.

Jocelyn was depressed about how different her life is now. She often wished things would go back to the way they used to be with her social circle. Jocelyn's family along with 3 other families spent a lot of time together vacationing, having parties, and celebrating holidays. She hosted many of these events and loved it. Their children basically grew up like siblings. The time came, however, when the children outgrew the family group thing. As late teens and young adults, the kids in the group discovered their own interests which did not include parents. And the parents of now grown children welcomed new couple experiences that did not involve the group of families.

So Jocelyn found herself lost. She did not adjust well to no longer having to plan for her friends' visits and sleepovers. Jocelyn interpreted these normal life changes to mean that her friends didn't enjoy her company anymore and stopped loving her. She was deeply sad and dwelled on how good things used to be when her group of friends was one big happy family.

In processing her sadness and depression, Jocelyn was able to recognize her losses in the changed group dynamic like fewer gatherings, absent and disinterested youngsters, less hosting, and diminished closeness with the other moms. In allowing herself to grieve, Jocelyn also realized that the declined invitations to events she wanted to host were not negatives about her, nor about her at all. Members of the other families, and even her own children, simply outgrew the dynamic and wanted to do something else with their time and energy.

Jocelyn learned that *no's* to her invitations were appropriate given her friends' changing priorities, and not a reflection of her worthiness—an emotional boundary issue. She was then able to accept that the past is the past, was able to remember those experiences without regret that they no longer existed, and successfully individuated from the group dynamic. And in doing so, Jocelyn discovered new and joyful relationships and couple activities with her husband.

SUMMARY

Understanding what anxiety and depression are and how they present enables you to manage them in such a way that minimizes their negative impact on you. You also empower yourself to set and affirm healthy boundaries to strengthen your resolve and resilience while limiting exposure to harmful forces that trigger or exacerbate depression and anxiety. This promotes your mental health.

CHAPTER 16

LIVING BOUNDARIES AND EMOTIONAL INTELLIGENCE

"Emotions are continually affecting our thought processes and decisions, below the level of our awareness. And the most common emotion of them all is the desire for pleasure and the avoidance of pain."
—Robert Greene

We humans have emotions. They are a natural part of the human experience. Yet, depending upon the culture and family dynamics, some emotions are acceptable while others are deemed signs of weakness and expression of them is forbidden. Typically, the only acceptable emotions are 'happiness' and love. Please note here that I conceptualize happiness as a description of a mental and emotional state that relies on the words and deeds of other people, not as an emotion itself. Rather, joy is the emotion that I see is an expression of your innate enthusiasm for life. Although joy can be triggered by the actions of others, it is available for you to experience all on your own. Think of the times when you smile and laugh while you are alone.

As a natural part of the Human Condition, emotions, all emotions, are necessary. You see, human emotions serve the purpose of delivering a message which is designed to enable the human being to become aware of, to address, and to consciously choose how to respond to the person or situation that triggered the emotion. Without the messages that emotions carry, you would not know when danger is around you, when you're experiencing a significant loss, nor when your boundaries have been violated.

My first book, *Living In Total Health*, breaks down the human emotional experience and shows how to unpack your emotional experiences so you can emote with intelligence. The Emoting with Intelligence chapter in *Living In Total* Health discusses 5 emotions, their derivatives (familiar names we call them), and how to unpack them to address the message each emotion attempts to deliver to you. These emotions are anger, sadness, fear, joy, and love.

Anger, sadness, and fear tend to be unpleasant and uncomfortable. The adults I work with most often try to ignore or suppress these emotions because the experience and expression of either was punished in some way by parents or others in positions of authority in their lives or because their role models used these emotions as excuses to harm themselves or others. Clients will even go so far as admonishing themselves for even experiencing anger, sadness, or fear because they see that just having these emotions is a personal defect. *"What's wrong with me? Why can't I stop feeling this way?"*

> *"Our job is to manage the physical manifestations, identify the underlying emotions and the messages they carry, and respond appropriately."*
> —*Living In Total Health*, Emoting with Intelligence Chapter

Addressing Anger

That brings us to anger. This emotion is often demonized and labeled as 'bad', typically because of how people use it. For example, batterers blame their abuse on anger, as if anger itself forced them to hit, kick, punch, or kill their romantic partner. Automatically acting out because of anger, as with the other emotions, is not an appropriate way to respond. It is a tantrum. Childish. Primitive.

Doing your emotional job effectively promotes personal growth and involves partnering the emotions with the intellect, hence the term *emotional intelligence.*

Anger gets triggered for different reasons. Some triggers include not having control over a person or situation, whether it's a realistic or unrealistic desire to control. Boundary violations also trigger anger. When you are in harm's way, when someone is attempting to impose their will upon you, and when someone betrays you, anger presents to motivate you to act and protect yourself.

Rather than beating yourself for being angry, your health and wellness require you to contain your anger, identify the anger trigger, identify the boundary issue, identify what your realm of control is, recognize if your anger is realistic or unrealistic, and make appropriate choices to respond to the trigger of your anger.

For the record, other words used to describe anger are irritation, annoyance, rage, hostility, upset, hurt, bitterness, resentment, fury, and frustration.

Let's look at a few examples of how managing anger plays out.

Example 1

Karla was frustrated that she didn't have a better relationship with her father. She described him as being aloof and disengaged whenever she was around him, which triggered her to cringe. Karla's frustration was unrealistic because she wanted to control how her father behaved with her, which she interpreted to be proof that she was unworthy and unlovable.

As we unpacked her anger, Karla recognized that there were things she could do in an attempt to improve the connection she had with her father. So she spent time watching TV with him, which he enjoyed, having coffee with him, and taking him to lunch.

After some time engaging in these activities, Karla realized that her father is aloof and distant with her because of who he is, and not because it was a reflection of her self-worth. So once Karla accepted who her father is, she stopped experiencing frustration in his presence and anger due to their limited connection. Karla successfully individuated (emotional boundary) from her father and alleviated her anger toward him.

Example 2

Casey's younger sister often went into Casey's room and took whatever she wanted—clothes, shoes, jewelry, books, etc. Casey repeatedly asked her sister to stop going into her room without consent and to ask for what she wanted rather than just take it. Her sister did not. Instead, she continued to violate Casey's personal and private space (mental boundary). So Casey was angry about it. Anger is naturally triggered by boundary violations.

Casey, seeing that her sister was unwilling to respect her private space, identified what she could do about it, responsibly. She chose to put a lock on her bedroom door to take away her sister's access.

Anger motivates and empowers.

Understanding Fear

Fear is another emotion that is misunderstood and often demonized. Realistic, healthy fear is necessary because it notifies you when you are in danger. Fear carries the message that actual danger is nearby which serves to elevate your awareness of your surroundings in case you need to act—fight, flee, or freeze. Think of my experience outside of T-Mobile arena from chapter 8 where I stood alone on a dark Las Vegas corner waiting for a rideshare pickup. My intuition alerted me to the potential danger nearby and motivated me to leave that spot just before a man walked up behind me. Without fear, I would not have walked away before the stranger approached my position and would've been completely vulnerable.

Another message offered by fear is that of the unknown. Anxiety and nervousness are naturally triggered by not knowing what's going to happen, even in positive situations. Remember walking across the graduation stage, being on a job interview, or getting married? I trembled just thinking about those events as they approached. Being nervous about them brought my attention to what I could control…focusing on my steps on stage and walking down the aisle, preparing answers to potential questions for the interview, and rehearsing my responses.

Example of unhealthy fear

Sarina and Mary have been romantic partners for six months. Mary often dismisses Sarina's opinion about many aspects of their relationship, like what to have for dinner or how to arrange furniture. Sarina wants to have a say about their life together. Yet, instead of having a conversation with Mary about it, Sarina continues to bite her tongue because she fears Mary's disapproval (emotional boundary).

Sarina is afraid to speak up for herself. This fear is not the life-threatening danger of being physically attacked nor the unknown involved in upcoming events as in the other examples above. Rather, Sarina turns her unhealthy fear on herself. *What's wrong with me? Why can't I just go along? Mary knows more than me so why can't I just listen and do what she says? If I keep acting like this then she is going to leave me.*

Sarina's unrealistic fear leads her to focus on what she can't control, Mary's responses, thereby increasing her anxiety that could potentially evolve into depression.

For the record, other words used to describe fear are anxious, afraid, nervous, panicked, scared, leary, frightened, and worried. Fear serves to identify danger around you and identify what you have personal control over.

Fear empowers.

Supporting Sadness

Sadness is necessary to properly process loss. Any time some one or some thing that you have an emotional investment in is no longer present in your life, you will grieve the loss. Grief is the process through which you release your mental and emotional attachment to who/what is no longer present in your life. And the loss can be about the death of a loved one, the death of someone you hated or feared, your best friend moving away, losing a job, and even your hope for someone, some thing, some situation. The grief process involves releasing your attachment through sadness.

While sadness isn't demonized in the same way as anger and fear are, it is still contested with platitudes. *You shouldn't be sad. It could be worse. You're still better off than most people. It wasn't that bad.* And because of this, you may shame yourself into ignoring your experience, suppressing your tears, or belittling the loss. By ignoring your innate need to properly grieve and experience appropriate sadness, mental unhealth looms. You see, unresolved grief can easily evolve into depression. Yet the more you allow your grief process to unfold, give yourself permission to experience sadness and tears when you're safe and have privacy, then your healing process will flow more smoothly.

For example, Carolyn discovered that her boyfriend was cheating on her. Infidelity is a deal breaker for her so she ended their relationship. Even though breaking up was Carolyn's decision, she was still very sad about it. And her friends telling her that she was better off without him did not alleviate the pain of losing someone she loved.

In therapy, Carolyn learned about the grief process. She also grew to understand that her sadness was a natural emotional response to losing something important, to the death of her relationship. Carolyn was then able to remember the good times with her boyfriend with diminishing sadness after she developed self-compassion and resilience.

For the record, other words used to describe sadness are down, blue, depressed, miserable, lost, melancholy, somber, sullen, and sorrow.

Sadness is empowering and healing.

Validating Love and Joy

This validation is about choosing healthy boundaries, the green flags. Boundary violations point to what is wrong in your relationship or situation. Red flags are precursors to these violations. Healthy boundaries, however, represent what is working for you along with the green light to continue and repeat the relevant choices and actions. The emotions love and joy are green flags that indicate what is working in your life, relationship, and situation, and serve to inspire you to repeat the actions that triggered them.

Love

Authentic connection is the cornerstone of true love. All forms of love, not just romantic love. Unadulterated love is the experience of being connected to your Personal Truth and to something more expansive than you are singularly—family, friends, community, creator. This type of love is-

> *"...all-encompassing love that surrounds us all the time like air. Imagine being wrapped in a warm blanket of support and acceptance every moment of every day. As with air, this experience of love is always accessible."*
> —Glen Alex, Living In Total Health

What connects you with yourself and others? Perhaps a self-care act like cooking your favorite meal and dining alone does it. Maybe the gratitude that comes with being able to help someone in need connects you. Or could it be that having warm, loving arms comfort and support you?

In teaching clients emotional intelligence, they all are able to recall feeling connected to others when they experience love.

For the record, other words used to describe love are warmth, fullness, and connection.

Joy

This emotion is your innate enthusiasm for life. I believe that each of us are born with the ability to be joyful in our own unique way. And no human can take it away because they didn't give it to you. Sure, sometimes we do lose sight of or disconnect from it when challenges arise. Joy is always available, however.

Note here that I differentiate joy from happiness. Being joyful is intrinsic to humanity and can be experienced alone. Happiness is more of a description of a moment that depends upon what other people say and do for you, which is always subject to what they are going through and what they choose at the time. Reliance on such makes you a puppet to others. And while joy can be triggered by people and events, it belongs to you.

Joy is also very grounding. Clients diagnosed with anxiety and depression do acknowledge that when they engage in joyful activities—reading, family activities, snuggling with pets, exercising, crafting, dancing, etc.—they are present and mindful in those moments without worry about the future and without lamenting the past.

For the record, other words used to describe joy are happy, elated, enthusiastic, content, delighted, pleasure, energetic, light, and fun.

What brings you joy? A silly commercial, completing a task, or possibly seeing children dance. It is crucial that you are aware of the green flags that tap into your love and joy so you can duplicate them.

All human emotions are necessary. Even the unpleasant and uncomfortable ones—anger, fear, sadness.

OTHER "EMOTIONS"

There seems to be some confusion between thoughts, feelings, and emotions. They are not the same. And for me, they are not interchangeable. So, I offer an alternate perspective on terms commonly identified as emotions.

> *"These other, pseudo-emotions are merely derivatives or combinations of the core ones. Or they aren't emotions at all. Some are thought processes."*
> —*Living in Total Health*, Emoting with Intelligence chapter

Guilt

Guilt arises from thinking you've done something wrong, made some kind of grave mistake. It can result from actual wrong-doing like, lying or taking someone else's belongings. Guilt can also arise from another person's negative outcomes, like a parent does when their adult child errs. The guilt is realistic or unrealistic. Either way, the experience is typically accompanied by anger, sadness, and/or fear.

In thinking you have messed up, it's important to differentiate between realistic versus unrealistic guilt. If your guilt is appropriate, meaning that you have actually done something wrong, the correction is in the guilt. Inherent in realistic guilt is the behavioral change for you to make in order to resolve your guilt and prevent repeating it.

Bill feels guilty for lying to his wife about spending $500 on a product even after they discussed and agreed to consulting each other before spending more than $300 on anything.

Corrective Action

- ✓ Bill doesn't lie to his wife.
- ✓ Bill keeps his agreement and doesn't spend more than $300 without talking with his wife first.

Unrealistic guilt, on the other hand, does not offer any solution to resolve the guilt because it is based upon personalization. This cognitive distortion is about you taking responsibility for negative events and negative consequences of other people's choices. And because there's no corrective action for you to take, the inappropriate guilt only serves as a negative, self-sustaining loop of proof that you're unworthy.

...father felt guilty for his adult son's truck getting repossessed because he failed as a parent.

Corrective Action

- ✓ None – the father can't control how his son chooses to manage his money even though he learned about finances in college.

Shame

The root of shame is the belief that you are an innately defective, broken, and flawed human being. It triggers a profound and intense fear of being exposed, that your defects are visible and that others can see there's something *wrong* with you.

> *"...shame is an underlying and pervasive belief that we are fundamentally inadequate, defective, and unacceptable—that who we are at our core is not worthy. Shame can make us believe that we're unlovable and don't belong; even worse, shame makes us overwhelmed with fear that others see our unworthiness and inadequacies as truth."*
> —Rubin Khoddam Ph.D.

Shame has been associated with imposter syndrome, which was first identified by researchers Pauline Rose Clance and Suzanne Ament Imes in 1978 from observing women who believed they achieved their PhDs and professional and academic excellence fraudulently. According to Therapist Danielle Wayne, imposter syndrome is the internalized *"intellectual phoniness"* of successful people who feel like they're deceiving others into thinking they're more intelligent or successful than they really are. More recently, imposter syndrome is reportedly experienced by all genders and in different settings.

Hate

Hate is based upon the firmly held belief that someone is a danger to you, fear that they will harm, defile, destroy, or extinguish you, your ilk, and your life as you know it. Those who hate are actually afraid that *they* will be permanently changed in a bad way by the object of their fear. Hate identifies whom to fear by relying primarily on their superficial traits such as skin color, physique, hair type. Then these traits are demonized and labeled as *bad, wrong, evil, unworthy, subhuman*. And the fear behind the hate is often masked by and is expressed as anger.

Hate creates the automatic, distorted thinking process that activates when those demonized, superficial traits are seen and is used to justify marginalizing, beating, abusing, and even killing those *scary* people.

SUMMARY

Human emotions are a natural part of the Human Condition. As such, the messages they carry are crucial because they call attention to issues that require us to address in order to live and be as safe and as healthy as possible. Some of those messages involve boundary violations, both internal and external. Acknowledging and accepting your emotional experiences puts you in position to best protect and nurture yourself.

CHAPTER 17

LIVING BOUNDARIES FOR DOING BUSINESS

"The worst thing you can do is meet expectations one time, fall short another, and exceed every now and then. I guarantee you'll drive your customers nuts and into the hands of the competition the first chance they get."
—Ken Blanchard and Sheldon Bowles

As healthy boundaries live and breathe within individuals, they are also impactful for business professionals. The professional needs good boundaries to attract and keep clients and customers, to earn goodwill, and to earn a positive reputation.

Here are a few tips for healthy boundaries in business.

1. Be On Time
   Poor time management is very frustrating for those who pay for products and services. This is a mental boundary issue because it involves agreements. I had a personal trainer who ran over twenty minutes with his client before me. Consequently, my session was limited to forty minutes while I was charged for sixty. The trainer explained that he didn't want to be rude and cut off the previous client. Yet he was okay with shortening my session by twenty minutes. My trainer could have demonstrated appropriate boundaries by informing the client before me that he had someone scheduled on the hour and finishing with them on time. I suggested he do so the first time because I should have

received the full hour for which I paid. He didn't, so I cancelled my contract the second time it happened.

Professionals must manage time and self in a way that respects themselves and their clients. And they must provide the client what they pay for. It's not cool that two clients each pay for a sixty-minute session, yet one client is allotted eighty minutes and the other forty. Many resources are available to assist with time and self-management. Start with the Stressing Less chapter in *Living In Total Health* to identify areas for you to improve.

In explaining the mental boundary and basic betrayal to clients, I use this example:

> Client A and therapist agreed to have sessions every week at 11:00 am. Yet, the therapist consistently arrives at 11:10 or 11:15. Over time, the client's frustration with the therapist's tardiness grows. When the client finally complains after 3 months, the therapist deflects and says, *"Well, I'm here now. So let's just make the best of the remaining time."*
>
> Poor Boundary
>
> ➤ The therapist is consistently late and betrays the agreement with her client to meet at 11:00. While it's acceptable to be late sometimes because of traffic or meetings running long, being late often violates the agreement of the mental boundary.
> ➤ The client allows the boundary violation to continue without speaking up is a poor boundary.
>
> Healthy Boundary

✓ The therapist makes appropriate adjustments to preparation and time management to arrive on time to each session.

✓ The client speaks up and addresses the therapist's tardiness sooner.

2. Keep Your Word

Time management isn't the only factor in credibility. Delivering what you promise is too. Keeping your word is not only the honorable and the right thing to do; it is a requirement for a favorable reputation. In this day of reviews on Yelp, Facebook, and other social media platforms, what people think of you is out there. Everyone around the world can see how you handle your business.

I know many people, myself included, who refused to use a contractor, nail tech, hair dresser, merchant, massage therapist, or dine at a restaurant after they failed to provide what they promised and advertised. According to Contented Cows, 78 percent of American consumers "abandoned a transaction or did not make a purchase that they had intended to make" because of poor customer service delivery.

More than that, "when consumers have a good customer experience, they tell an average of nine people about it. But when they have a negative experience, they tell twice as many people about it. Add to that the interconnectedness of today's consumers through various social media platforms, and that could spell big trouble when negative comments go viral."

After moving to a new city, I established care with a new medical provider. During my 2nd annual physical, he said he would refer me for a medical test and Gastroenterology (GI) assessment to rule out conditions he was concerned about. He ordered the test immediately and I completed it within a couple of days. About a week later, I called the GI's office to confirm receipt of the referral. They had not received it. So, I called my provider's office to follow up on the test results and the referral. The shared receptionist said she'd give the provider my message.

No return call nor any referral was made. I repeatedly checked on the referral by calling the GI clinic and I called my provider's office regarding my test results. Still no response. I then emailed and left voicemail messages on the provider's cell phone. This provider did not respond to me, therefore he failed to keep his word. Because of his betrayal, not keeping the agreement he made with me, I switched providers.

Not only was the provider above guilty of patient abandonment when he didn't respond or keep his word with me, he failed to communicate any issues with making the GI referral and with reviewing my test results that had me worried. Had he let me know that insurance changed its referral procedures and the referral would take longer than he anticipated or the GI clinic was no longer accepting referrals or that he was going on vacation, then I would have been more understanding and patient with him.

3. Communicate
   Effective communication can lead to repeat business, referrals, and increased sales. Companies that fail to respond to calls or messages, either voicemail or email, usually don't do so well. Entrepreneur.com reported that most customers contact businesses via telephone, even in this age of technology. Only 3 percent of contact is made on social media platforms. So with that in mind, here are a few recommendations for effective communication strategies.

- ✓ First impressions matter. So, answering professionally and having a professional message greeting go a long way toward customer retention. Eighty-three percent of customers surveyed said they avoid a company or stop doing business with it after a poor phone experience, according to businessnewsdaily.com.
- ✓ Speak to clients with authenticity, like they are real people. Discard the patented generic responses that convey false empathy and address each customer's specific issue or concern. I get so annoyed by customer service reps who pretend to understand and care. The best way to show you care is to actually address the problem quickly and efficiently, and not just say you will.

4. Behavior outside the office

Business owners and staff continue to represent the business even when off duty. And small business owners are the physical representation of the product or service they offer.

> *"Respect the personal boundaries of everyone...you*
> *encounter in your work and daily life. An*
> *entrepreneur's reputation does not have a time clock*
> *so how you behave outside of work counts too."*
> —Glen Alex, *Living In Total Health* Boundaries Chapter

I met a certified health and life coach at a networking event. At that time, I promoted my massage therapy business. When she heard that I was a Massage Therapist, she said, *"I bet you touch a lot of hot bodies."* She then openly shared how she fantasizes about her attractive clients and had even dated a few of them.

I found her poor professional and personal boundaries disturbing. Not only did she get romantically involved with her clients, which many licensing and certification regulatory bodies forbid, her oversharing and enmeshment were off-putting to me. Right then and there I decided to refer anyone I knew in need of coaching to someone else.

SUMMARY

It is very important for business owners and staff to be professional at all times in public spaces. Sure, there are times and situations when owners and employees want to let their guard down and get loose. Understandable. In private. Whatever your personal inclinations are, maintain appropriate boundaries when anyone can see you. Remember the CEO and the human resources manager who were caught on the Kiss Cam in an intimate position at a recent Cold Play concert? The video of it went viral because of their reactions of shame. They both were married to someone else. What credibility did either of them have after that?

And with this new understanding of boundaries for business, customers can hold the professionals they hire and contract with accountable for how they conduct business.

SECTION IV

CHAPTER 18

RE-ASSESSING YOUR LINE IN THE SAND

"You can be a good person with a kind heart and still say no to people."
—Tracy Malone

This is a great time to re-assess your boundaries to see what you've learned and how the new information will impact the boundaries you set and affirm.

As before, simply respond to the statements and questions below as honestly as you can. Please do not look back to your previous responses to avoid bias. The more present and genuine you are, then the more clear your boundaries will be.

Feel free to share your self-assessment with your therapist, counselor, or life coach to aid your progress in setting and maintaining appropriate boundaries for your mental health and overall wellness.

1. Saying *no* makes you strong?
    □ Yes   □ No   □ It should

2. Boundaries only apply to sexual situations?
    □ Yes   □ No

3. Setting boundaries is the "in thing"?
    □ Yes   □ No

4. Having healthy boundaries help with stress?
   □ Yes   □ No   □ Makes stress worse

5. People will accept when you say *no?*
   □ Yes   □ No   □ They should

6. Do you overcommit to what family and friends want?
   □ All the time   □ A lot   □ Sometimes   □ No

7. Do you have trouble separating your thoughts and emotions from someone else?
   □ All the time   □ Sometimes   □ Never

8. Do you allow people to stand closer than you're comfortable with?
   □ Yes   □ No   □ Sometimes

9. Do you provide more information than the conversation requires?
   □ All the time   □ Sometimes   □ Never

10. How often do you apologize for being late or not following through on something?
    □ All the time   □ A lot   □ Sometimes   □ Rarely

11. Are you an open book?
    □ Yes   □ No

12. How often do you give in and do something you don't want to do?
    □ All the time   □ Sometimes   □ Never

13. Does how people treat you align with your beliefs and values?
  □ Yes   □ No

14. How comfortable are you saying "no"?
  □ Very   □ Somewhat   □ Not at all

15. How do you handle unwanted touching?
  □ Back away   □ Speak up   □ Wait for it to end

16. Do you follow someone else's lead when you don't want to?
  □ All the time   □ Sometimes   □ Never

17. People who care about you should know what you want and need?
  □ Yes   □ I think so   □ No   □ I'm not sure

18. Do you agree just to get along?
  □ All the time   □ A lot   □ Sometimes   □ Rarely

19. Do you sacrifice your self-care to do what others want you to do?
  □ All the time   □ A lot   □ Sometimes   □ No

20. Do you have trouble making time for self-care?
  □ Yes   □ No   □ Sometimes

Now that you have reassessed your boundaries, answer the following questions:

What changed for you?

_____

What's your new understanding of boundaries?

_____

Did your strengths change?

_____

Did your areas of improvement change?

_____

Use this Boundaries Assessment to assist you in developing your Declarations of Your Line in The Sand.

CHAPTER 19

DECLARING YOUR LINE IN THE SAND

*"Boundaries are the adult version of 'You're not
allowed in my treehouse!'"*
—Unknown

This is the declaration of your line in the sand.

I,_____, hereby declare that as a Human adult with inherent worth, I have the innate and unalienable right to protect myself from harmful forces, people, and situations. I also have the right to nurture my uniqueness.

1. I exercise my innate right to determine what I tolerate, from whom, when, and for how long.
2. I exercise my innate right to choose my own path.
3. I exercise my innate right to define my own reality.
4. I exercise my innate right to advocate for my health and well-being.
5. I exercise my innate right to communicate my boundaries.
6. I exercise my innate right to apply appropriate consequences for violations of my boundaries.
7. I exercise my innate right to end a relationship or leave a situation in response to any of my deal breakers, which can include:
   1). Abuse
   2). Lying
   3). Infidelity
   4). Betrayal

5). Stealing

8. I exercise my innate right to express my emotions and feel what I feel when I feel it.

9. I exercise my innate right to express my needs and opinions appropriately.

10. I exercise my innate right to have a community of family, friends, spiritual leaders, mentors, and other loved ones of my choosing.

11. I exercise my innate right to prioritize my self-care.

12. I exercise my innate right to adjust and alter my boundaries as needed.

Use the lines below to add your own declarations.

_____

_____

_____

_____

_____

_____

A FINAL NOTE

"Boundaries are the foundation of health and happiness."
—Glen Alex, LCSW, Author of *Living In Total Health*

My goal for writing *Living Boundaries* is for you to learn about all aspects of boundaries, which involve much more than just saying 'no'. The process of identifying, setting, maintaining, and affirming your boundaries enables you to honor and express your innate uniqueness, gifts, and talents. This process also protects the integrity of your humanity while opening your heart and mind to authentic love and joy.

Without healthy boundaries, disrespect, abuse, and other forms of mistreatment not only occur, they can persist. Depression, anxiety, stress, overwhelm, toxic relationships, loneliness, self-loathing, self-harm, and other issues and conditions take over your life. Pain and suffering become constants.

In my first published book, the 5-time award-winning *Living In Total Health*, I introduced the concept of WELLTH, which I defined as health plus other riches. Wellth is the foundation of my work in the health and wellness and psychology spaces. This transformative mission that guides my work is to help as many people as I can be joyful, connected, confident, and complete—Wellthy.

Healthy boundaries are an absolute requirement for Wellth. Boundaries live and breathe with us humans, providing intuition, insights, and empowering choices for us to protect and nurture ourselves. I firmly believe that this will lead to wholeness and authentic love and joy.

Please consider that if more people developed healthy boundaries, then there would be less violence, less oppression, and fewer isms. *Living Boundaries* are key to the world being safer, more accepting, and more loving for all humans. And *Living Boundaries* are the responsibility of all members of the human race--women, men, those with non-traditional lifestyles, politicians, leaders, business people, doctors, lawyers, law enforcers, customers, parents.

So take ownership and be personally accountable for your boundaries. Read and reread *Living Boundaries,* complete the assessments and exercises, practice what you learn, and share *Living Boundaries* with your loved ones.

> *"Boundaries are the distance at which I can love you*
> *and myself at the same time."*
> —Prentis Hemphill

EXCERPT FROM LIVING IN TOTAL HEALTH

BY GLEN ALEX

Keep reading for an excerpt from Glen's first published book, the 5-time award-winning *Living In Total Health: Reconnecting with Your Wellth*. Because humans are social creatures and interpersonal boundaries set the parameters for interaction, it is most appropriate to share an excerpt from the Relating Well Chapter.

If you want to learn more about boundaries, total health, and your wholeness, then order *Living In Total Health* on www.GlenAlex.com. It is available in hardcover, paperback, and ebook.

LIVING IN TOTAL HEALTH:
Reconnecting with Your Wellth

RELATING WELL

"The beginning of love is to let those we love be perfectly themselves, and not to twist them to fit our own image. Otherwise we love only the reflection of ourselves we find in them."
—Thomas Merton

Humans are social creatures. We need to relate to others to understand self and to feel "whole." Our relationships occur on multiple levels—familial, intimate, and friendship. We even learn about ourselves from coworkers, teachers, and anyone with whom we share time and energy. Relationships are either healthy or unhealthy, either adding to or hindering insight. Either they nurture personal growth and wellth or inhibit them. The nurturing and mutual respect elements in these relationships create an environment in which the partners thrive personally and grow with one another. And individuals in any healthy relationship respect the uniqueness of each other.

Let me give you an example. I had a coworker in Texas. She and I related comfortably shortly after meeting. Katy was funny, smart, and open-minded, as was I, so we clicked. About a year into our friendship, I stood at her desk while we talked about which movie we would go see together. Katy suggested, Indecent Proposal. I was being me, so I honestly said, "I don't want to see that." "Why not?" she asked. "Because I don't agree with the premise of the movie so I won't enjoy it." You would have thought that I threatened to sell her favorite child into prostitution because her reaction was so extreme. Katy started yelling and saying things like "You think you're better than everybody else, and you...and you...and you....." I retorted that I had only expressed my opinion and wasn't implying that she shouldn't see the movie. Katy never spoke to me again. Whoa!

In retrospect, Katy always valued my opinion when we agreed. However, I didn't realize that my own uniqueness wasn't respected in our relationship until I had a viewpoint different from her own. Not a healthy situation. The cornerstones of unhealthy relationships are exhibited when one partner dominates the other, when one partner fantasizes that relationships develop automatically from attraction and without concerted effort, and when one partner punishes the other for not fulfilling expectations. My guess is that Katy felt betrayed by my diverse opinion, which she did not expect, then punished me for it by ending our friendship.

UNDERSTANDING

Inherent in healthy relationships is the very undervalued trait of understanding. Each partner has or develops the ability to try to understand the other's perspective, especially when there is disagreement. These partners inquire, discuss, and listen, knowing that understanding is not agreement. Instead, seeing another person's point of view is empathy that adds great value and intimacy. Unfortunately, Katy was not interested in understanding my opinion.

"Seek first to understand, then to be understood." I first heard this statement from my ex-husband. He had learned it in Narcotics Anonymous during treatment prior to our meeting. Unfortunately, it only applied to his being understood by me so he could do whatever he wanted.

Individuals in a relationship may have the unrealistic expectation that their love (even love in non-intimate relations) for their partner is all that is needed. They assume that their partners will satisfy their unspoken and unmet psychological and emotional needs and will always be available to them. Unspoken and unrealistic expectations kill relationships.

RELATING CONSCIOUSLY

Relating in this unrealistic way is what Harville Hendrix, Ph.D., the author of *Getting the Love You Want*, calls "unconscious." Although the meat of his work is with intimate couples, much of it applies to other types of partnerships as well. All relationships share the phases of:

1. Attraction—a smile, a comment, a joke, a gesture like holding a door open

2. Make believe—pretense to make a good impression

3. Denial—ignoring/overlooking the other's negative traits

4. Projection—attributing one's disowned parts of self onto the other

5. Power struggle—the "honeymoon" phase is over and tactics are employed to coerce your partner to satisfy your unrealistic and unspoken expectations

6. Make or break it—either partners will grow together or the relationship degenerates

When times get tough, which is a natural part of life, unconscious partners expect that the love (the partner) will work it out, ignoring that each person has work to do—inquire, discuss, listen.

According to Hendrix, traits of a conscious relationship are:

1. You realize your partnership has a hidden purpose beyond your superficial needs and desires. Unresolved childhood issues lie beneath the surface and daily interactions have deeper meaning.

2. You create a more realistic image of your partner and let go of the illusions that your partner will save you.

3. You take responsibility for your own needs and desires and communicate them appropriately and stop expecting your partner to automatically fulfill you.

4. Your actions become conscious, intentional and constructive, rather than reactive.

5. You learn to appreciate your partner's needs as much as you value your own, less narcissism and more empathy.

6. You embrace the dark side of your personality by openly acknowledging your negative traits and accepting responsibility for them.

7. You learn new techniques to meet your own basic needs and stop trying to coerce (blame, threaten, cajole) your partner to do it. You realize that your partner is a resource.

8. You search within for strengths and abilities that you lack. You come to see that your sense of "wholeness" is about developing your hidden skills and not through your partner "completing" you.

9. You begin to reconnect with your original nature to love unconditionally and experience unity with the world and wholeness.

10. You accept the work needed to create a good relationship. You realize that good relations mean being the right partner rather than picking the right partner.

On the other hand, negative or toxic relations are unhealthy when partners are not valued. Rather, these harmful relationships entail disrespect of one partner; they retard and negate growth, confining the less dominant partner to a box controlled by the more dominant partner.

Stephen Covey in *The 7 Habits of Highly Effective People* talks about the Emotional Bank Account. Similar to a financial bank account, healthy relationships require more deposits than withdrawals. The goal is to invest more love and kindness in your partner than whatever it is you get out of him or her. Deposits include understanding, hugs, sincere compliments, and loving honesty. These acts communicate that "My goal is your happiness," for example. Covey also says that "Love is a verb." Love is action, feeling in motion. Behavior is far more telling and indicative of underlying emotions and motives than words.

By contrast, withdrawals are obvious—unconstructive criticism, any form of abuse, ridicule, deception, and manipulation. Withdrawals take away from connection and create deficits. These hurtful behaviors impact the core of the relationship and undermine the recipient partner's trust.

WHOM WE ATTRACT

We attract our ilk. Like begets like. The old adage "opposites attract" is not completely accurate. We are programmed to gravitate toward validation of our beliefs and values. So relationally, we seek that too. And every person in our chosen relationships is a mirror, reflecting back different aspects of our emotional needs. "Opposites" to me mean the outward expressiveness of individuals. On the inside, both partners have the same level of emotional maturity. They just show it differently.

During my work in domestic violence, I worked on both sides of the fence with the battered and the batterer. I discovered a great misnomer about this important social issue. Yes, the women are dependent on the men and some cannot fathom their existence without the batterer, no matter how dangerous he is to them and their children. The same is also true for the batterer, which is rarely mentioned. His psychological existence is just as dependent on her as hers is on him. For without her as the object to project his self-loathing and anger, he cannot exist. Think of the batterer as a movie projector and the woman he abuses as the screen that displays his film. Without the screen, the projector is idle and without meaning. Yes, he needs her too.

Yet batterers typically blame the women they abuse for their violence: "She made me do it." Such statements are common from abusers who want to sidestep responsibility for their actions. So my question is: If the woman drives him to such barbarity, then why doesn't he leave? Unfortunately, society only focuses on why she won't leave him.

During a batterers' treatment group that I facilitated with another therapist, one batterer complained about how his wife did a certain thing wrong, wasn't good in that way, and provoked him. He really sounded unhappy. So I asked, "Why don't you leave?" He fell silent as confusion settled on his face.

The character traits of the batterer and the battered woman present themselves as opposites. He typically is aggressive and she typically is passive. On the inside, however, they both are dependent and afraid to be alone. Thus, instead of attracting an opposite, we attract our complement—someone whose personality meshes/fits with ours, like pieces of a puzzle.

However complementary, unhealthy relationships are damning. They tarnish the heart and kill the spirit. Instead of growing together and deepening connectedness, these toxic relationships are disconnecting and isolative.

The son of a friend lamented about not being in a relationship with the person he pursued. Randy, in his early twenties, said that he had become the person he thought the object of his desire wanted him to be and he cried in agony when that person rejected him still.

Randy struggled to be something he wasn't, hoping for a false payoff. Not surprisingly, he failed. He went against his nature. Doing so almost always results in failure. It is impossible to be fake (be someone else) and attain something genuine (love).

> *"Some of the biggest challenges in relationships come from the fact that most people enter a relationship in order to get something: they're trying to find someone who's going to make them feel good. In reality, the only way a relationship will last is if you see your relationship as a place that you go to give, and not a place that you go to take."*
> —Anthony Robbins

SUMMARY

Healthy relationships have a very specific theme—an underlying current of mutual respect and nurturing that forms the foundation of all interactions. Hence, relating well means being open to experience your partner's truth, feeling free to share your true self, taking responsibility for your own happiness, and communicating your needs in a way that does not blame the other person for your stuff.

ABOUT THE AUTHOR

Glen Alex's life's work is about total health. Glen believes that a healthy body, mind, and spirit are collectively the full expression of humanity. So, health is at the forefront of her life. Whether in writing, podcasting, social work, charity work, tennis, or interpersonal relations, Glen puts her healthiest foot forward to make overall health and wellness the primary focus of her endeavors because of her lifelong belief in health as the ticket to personal empowerment and growth, connection to God, and connection to joy.

Health became a passion for Glen early on, beginning with boundaries. The first inkling she had about health was in personal relationships. Glen is the youngest of ten children, seven girls and three boys, and she learned a lot from observing how others around her behaved toward one another. She was very attentive to the nuances and dynamics of the person-to-person interactions and the environment around her. Glen absorbed meanings not apparent to the naked eye or the physical senses.

Witnessing the relational dynamics among family members, friends, teachers, Glen was so engaged by the nuance of interaction—when people smiled, laughed, cringed, and when pain crossed their faces. She determined as a child that deliberately negative interactions cause pain to others, and she decided she would not emulate them. Glen clearly remembers vowing to not be the aggressor and cause another person's pain. She saw boundaries respected and boundaries violated in real time, and it stuck. Glen then filtered her relational experiences and those she was privy to and categorized them. From that, Glen's work expanded as other areas of health revealed themselves to her and she developed a unique and no-nonsense perspective to help others lead their healthiest and most joyful life.

In working with clients and others, Glen's transformative mission is to help as many people as possible be joyful, connected, confident, and complete, the life experience she calls Wellth, which is health + other riches. Glen currently provides mental health therapy and Wellth Counseling virtually, and speaks on matters of health. Glen strives to spread health to others with pertinent and immediately actionable information that empowers them to make the best conscious choices about their health.

Professionally, Glen's experience is well-rounded in health and wellness. She is the author of the award-winning book *Living In Total Health*, a Licensed Clinical Social Worker, a Licensed Massage Therapist, Racquet Sports Professionals Association (RSPA) Certified Tennis Coach, Burnalong Instructor, Founder and Executive Director of former G. Alex Foundation, Marquis Who's Who Inductee, and Host of the award-winning podcast, The Glen Alex Show.

Glen Alex is a contributing author in the following publications:

❖ *Wellness Through Words* Anthology: <u>Living Well with Boundaries</u> Chapter, 2024

- ❖ *Messages Straight From The Heart - Stories of Inspiration from Nevada*, 2014
- ❖ Journal of Community Practice, 2001 Volume 9, Number 4

Glen's career highlights include:

- ★ 2025 Firebird Book Awards for Health & Wellness and Body, Mind, Spirit
- ★ 2025 Corporate Vision Mental Health Educator of the Year
- ★ 2024 Marquis Who's Who Inductee
- ★ 2023 USTA Champion of Equality Intermountain
- ★ 2023 Book Excellence Award for Health
- ★ 2023 Positive Change Podcast Awards for Health & Wellness and Psychology
- ★ 2021 Next Generation Indie Book Awards for Health & Wellness and Body, Mind, Spirit
- ★ 2010-2007 Personal Massage Therapist for the Bryan Brothers
- ★ 2009-2018 USTA Nevada, USTA Intermountain, USPTA Intermountain Awards for service in professional and recreational tennis
- ★ 1996 Creator of the Violence Intervention Program for Women

Glen currently lives in Oregon with her husband, Ben, and 2 cats. When not working in one of her many careers, Glen enjoys writing, playing tennis, working out, watching movies, listening to music, and connecting with loved ones.

For more information about Glen Alex, visit her at:
https://glenalex.com/

WORKING WITH GLEN

"Glen is by far the best therapist I have had. She continually adapts her sessions to help guide me through whatever I have going on in life whether it's related to work, school, or my family. I'm always excited for my sessions with her because I am continuing to learn about myself and feel closer to person I want to become with each session."
—Leanne M

Glen Alex respects the humanity of all clients, whether they are mental health therapy or Wellth Counseling clients. From that perspective, Glen is able to connect with clients where they are and support their growth and healing process on a profound level. The issues Glen works with clients on include boundaries, anxiety, depression, stress, overwhelm, burnout, relationships, chronic illness, communication, work-related distress, family, parenting, emotional intelligence, and grief.

Validating the inherent worth of each client, Glen provides a safe and supportive space for clients to express themselves, share their pain, be accountable, learn coping skills, and empower themselves. In treatment, clients will receive Glen's no-nonsense approach to mental health therapy and Wellth Counseling to learn skills to cope with life challenges and experience themselves in healthier ways.

In addition to *Living In Total Health,* The Glen Alex Show podcast, and blogs, Glen has developed Wellth tools to assist clients in achieving self-awareness, mindfulness, mental flexibility, grounding, and other healthy coping skills. Glen's Wellth tools include The Stress Less Box, a journal notebook, Nutrients 4 Muscle Health Guide, and handouts.

Currently, Glen provides virtual sessions on multiple platforms to increase clients' access to her services. She accepts over 150 insurances and self-pay clients. Glen also offers complimentary consultations to assess a client's treatment needs and to determine if she and the client are a good fit for working together.

To request your complimentary consultation with Glen, visit https://glenalex.com/.

BOOK GLEN TO SPEAK AT YOUR NEXT EVENT

"I enjoy your energy and enthusiasm to share why you love what you do. All of the experiences you shared were educational."
—Marianne S.

In choosing a professional speaker for your next event, you'll find Glen to be dynamic, respected, and successful. She will leave your audience or colleagues with such a renewed passion for health and life that they will leave committed to making true life changes. For more than twenty years, Glen has worked with individuals and groups in different fields to facilitate their engagement and commitment to health.

No matter if your audience is ten or ten thousand, in North America or abroad, Glen Alex can deliver a tailor-made message of inspiration for your meeting or conference. Glen's speaking philosophy is that your audience does not want to be "taught" anything. Rather they are interested in hearing stories of inspiration, achievement, and real-life people achieving their goals, which will motivate them to do the same.

If you are looking for a memorable speaker who will leave your audience wanting more, then book Glen Alex today.

To see a highlight video of Glen and learn whether she is available for your next meeting, visit her site below and then contact her to schedule a complimentary pre-speech interview by phone:

https://glenalex.com/ Glen@ GlenAlex.com
702.577.0428

www.ingramcontent.com/pod-product-compliance
Lightning Source LLC
Chambersburg PA
CBHW071737120626
46550CB00002B/552